Withdrawn from
Queen Margaret University Library

Reflections

on

Relaxation

over one hundred and fifty stress-reducing ideas

Judy Loosmore

illustrations by
Lynne Thompson

Detselig Enterprises Ltd.
Calgary, Alberta, Canada

QUEEN MARGARET COLLEGE LIBRARY

Reflections on Relaxation

© 1994 Judy Loosmore

Canadian Cataloguing in Publication Data

Loosmore, Judith M. (Judith Marjory), 19**-
  Reflections on relaxation

  Includes bibliographical references.

  ISBN 1-55059-081-2

  1. Relaxation. 2. Stress management. I. Title.
  RA785.L66 1994   613.7'9   C94-910237-7

Publisher's Data

Detselig Enterprises Ltd.
210, 1220 Kensington Road NW
Calgary, Alberta T2N 3P5

Detselig Enterprises Ltd. appreciates the financial support for our 1994 publishing program, provided by the Department of Communications, Canada Council and the Alberta Foundation for the Arts, a beneficiary of the Lottery Fund of the Government of Alberta.

Edited by Sherry Wilson McEwen

Cover design by Dean MacDonald

All rights reserved. No part of this book may be reproduced in any form or by any means without permission in writing from the publisher.

Printed in Canada   ISBN 1-55059-0-81-2   SAN 115-0324

This book is dedicated with love, peace and joy to my parents, my sister, and my love . . .

And with many thanks to my many friends who encouraged and helped me.

Other books in the *Life Line* series:

Contents

Introduction

Inside this book you will find a potpourri of ideas and suggestions to help relieve the effects of everyday stress and tension. You won't find definitions of stress or information on how stress affects the body and mind (there are lots of good books available on this subject).

You *will* find a lot of wonderful methods for coping with stress – everything from a positive self-talk or a romantic bubble bath to learning how to juggle or taking a walk.

What causes stress or tension is different for each of us. You may be totally comfortable doing something that would cause me discomfort and vice versa. How we deal with stress and tension in our lives is also very personal. Stress reduction should be something YOU enjoy doing; something that relaxes YOU. Because it's so personal, a potpourri of coping techniques are offered. Some of them will work for you and others won't. Some will work for you sometimes but not at other times. Pick and choose, mix and match. Have fun experimenting.

God, grant me the serenity to accept the things I cannot change; the courage to change the things I can; and the wisdom to know the difference.
–The Serenity Prayer

To yield is to be preserved whole,
To bend is to become straight.
To be empty is to be full.
To be worn out is to be renewed.
To have little is to possess.
– Lao-Tzu

First keep the peace within yourself, then you can also bring peace to others.
– Thomas à Kempis

Perfect bliss grows only in the heart made tranquil.
– Hindu Proverb

Note: If you have major stress problems, consult your doctor. This book is intended to help you cope with everyday stresses only. If you have major distress, it will be better for you to seek professional help.

Sometimes relaxation is accomplished through an activity. At other times, a passive role is preferable. Sometimes simply managing to be alone in a quiet place for five minutes may be all the coping strategy you need. At other times, you will prefer to be with others.

Depending upon the situation, you may want a lot of your senses involved or very few. If your nerves are jangled then you may want to limit sensory input. Personally, when I'm really at the edge, peace and quiet are about the only things that help. And when I really let myself go beyond the point of no return before giving myself a break, the only thing that helps is a nap (my version of making the world go away for awhile). Upon awakening refreshed, I am better able to deal with things. At other times, when some problem is bothering me, becoming involved with something that focuses my attention elsewhere is what gets me through. Often, I find I can come back to the problem with a fresher and calmer perspective.

Frequently, what helps is to consciously stop worrying about potentially disastrous outcomes and focus on the potentially positive ones (which are usually more realistic). To stop snowballing anxious thoughts, deliberately sit down, take four deep breaths and visualize a calm and positive outcome based on reality. For example, if I'm concerned about delivering a presentation, I will visualize myself taking four deep breaths and walking graciously to the podium. I then visualize the presentation going smoothly with the audience demonstrating an interest in the topic. As the visualization progresses, I see myself at the end of the presentation with the audience applauding and me walking calmly off. It works for me, so I use it.

The ideas presented in this book are methods which can be used at home, at work, or away from both locations. These ideas were not developed to help you find new and improved ways to procrastinate! They are methods which have worked for me and others to help us become focused, grounded and revitalized and therefore able to cope with everyday stresses.

At the back of the book is a reference list of sources indicating useful tapes, books and visuals. This list is a starting place only. It is by no means exhaustive. Its intent is to guide you in your own journey toward stress reduction.

The stress-reducing techniques are presented in six chapters. Each chapter has space for you to fill in your own ideas in the margins. The chapters are: ACTIVATE (to get your blood moving), CREATE (to help you use those creative energies within you), SURROUND (your living/working environment can help to relieve stress), LEARN (to get your mind focused on exciting new ventures and thoughts), REFRESH (to help you to feel good about yourself and life in general) and CARE FOR (your emotional and physical health). The ideas within each chapter are presented in alphabetical order.

I hope you enjoy this book as it guides you in developing your own repertoire of stress-coping techniques. If you have any wonderful ideas for coping with stress that you would like to share, I'd appreciate hearing from you. Please write to:

Judy Loosmore
P.O. Box 63009
2604 Kensington Road N.W.
Calgary, Alberta, Canada
T2N 4S5

Activate

*True enjoyment comes from activity of the mind
and exercise of the body;
the two are ever united.*
– Humboldt

Activate

This section provides ideas for stress releasing techniques which require *energy*. They range from quick actions such as belting out your favorite song to more time-consuming activities such as playing a round of golf or going for a horseback ride.

It is now well-known that exercise helps to relieve stress. So, get up and get going!

Camping

Being awakened by the sun. Smelling the wonderfully clean pine air. Stretching to reach the morning sky. Camping can be marvelous. I adore the scent of a wood fire (unless I'm downwind of the smoke and unable to breathe). There is nothing quite like those flaming toasted marshmallows – crispy black on the outside and oh so gooey and stick-to-your-fingers in the middle. And the night sky is absolutely glorious with its zillions of stars.

Dance

There is something gracious about ballroom dancing. If you get a chance to learn this art, take it. The flowing move-

Never let your energy get blocked. You gain energy by exerting energy, so whenever you feel blue do something active.
– Alexandra Stoddard

Among the scenes which are impressed on my mind, none exceed in sublimity the primeval forests undefaced by the hand of man . . . no one can stand in solitudes unmoved, and not feel that there is more in man than the mere breath of his body.
– Charles Darwin

Are not the mountains, waves, and skies, a part Of me and my soul, as I of them?
– Lord Byron

ments and uplifting music are relaxing for eyes, ears, body and soul.

Belly dancing is excitingly exotic. Sorry, men, I've never seen a male belly dancer. Of course, there's a first time for everything. The sensual movements of this style of dance can bring a sense of peace.

The place of the dance is within the heart.
– Tom Robbins

Folk dancing is one of my favorites. Folk dance music has a spirit all its own. Line dances, circle dances, couple dances and mixers are all fun. The power and excitement of the music of various countries make your feet move in spite of themselves. I can be "beat" when I arrive at a dance but am soon energized by the movements and the music.

Will you, won't you,
will you, won't you,
will you join the dance?
– Lewis Carroll

"Just for yourself" dancing is the absolute best! Put on your favorite piece of music and let yourself go. Twirl. Leap. Boogey. Sing along. I highly recommend privacy for this activity unless you really trust those with you. If you become the least bit self-conscious while participating in this, you will probably stop immediately and possibly quit doing it forever. However, if you do have some friends around and you are all in a goofy mood, go for it! It's also great fun with children.

Exercise

If you are not a regular exerciser and are contemplating embarking upon an exercise program, see your doctor first. There are many places which offer fitness appraisals. I recommend going for one if it's been a while since you exercised.

Nothing assaults the conscience like an unused exercise bike.
— Ivern Ball

My friend Charmaine made herself a New Year's resolution in the mid-1980s to exercise a certain amount every week. She kept the amount of time per week achievable for herself and her lifestyle. She also kept the resolution flexible; it could be any kind of exercise from aerobics to swimming to walking, as long as she maintained the exercise for a minimum of twenty minutes a session. She is still exercising today. Except for illness, she has not missed a week.

Aerobics

Get out to the gym or put that tape or television program on and move to the sounds. Don't worry if you are unable to keep up or match the movements exactly. Just move in the way that releases your stress. Relish your accomplishments.

In your shirt and your socks (the black silk with gold clocks), crossing Salisbury Plain on a bicycle.
– W.S. Gilbert

Biking

This can be outdoors on a moving bicycle or indoors on a stationary bike. The outdoor bike could be seasonal depending upon the climate in which you live. Personally, I would find nothing relaxing about riding a bike, even a mountain bike, on snowy roads with temperatures below zero. I also find it stressful riding in high-traffic areas or totally concrete areas. But for some people, this is merely a challenge!

Try to cycle near natural areas. My city, Calgary, is blessed with numerous bike paths, many of which are in parkland. If your area doesn't have this option, try cycling in a residential area where you can enjoy the beauty of people's gardens and landscaping. If you are using a stationary bike, you might want to try adding music to your ride.

Lynne, the illustrator of this book, has a friend who manages to get her daily exercise by allowing herself to watch her favorite television program *only* if she rides her stationary bike at the same time.

Browse

Try browsing in art galleries, book-
stores, card shops, tropical fish stores,
flower shops, kitchen stores, museums
or toy stores.

Let your senses become involved when
you browse. Stop to look, smell, feel.
For example, whenever I walk into a
flower shop, I breathe in the moist cool
air. I can almost feel my skin rejoicing. I
enjoy browsing and talking with the flo-
rist about the names of various flowers
or plants and how to look after them. I
can rarely walk out of a flower shop
without buying at least a single perfect
rose. All the way home I anticipate how
it will look and feel and smell.

*What with the excellent
browsing and sluicing and
cheery conversation and
what-not the afternoon
passed quite happily.*
– P.G. Wodehouse

If you are browsing in stores, you might
want to make sure your credit cards remain at home. Look at the items in the
stores in a different way. Forget the
price tags. Look at toys and children's
books for the fun of it. Locate items that
made you happy as a child and handle
them again. Pick up that art book and
gently leaf through it.

Take your time in the art gallery and decide which picture or sculpture you
would choose for your home or office.

Jog/Run/Walk

Be sensible about this. If the area in which you might be jogging, running or walking isn't totally safe, the activity will not be a stress reliever. Also watch the timing of your outing. If you decide to run in the wee hours of the morning because it helps you get to sleep, then maybe you should consider an indoor activity such as aerobics or dancing instead. It has become a fact of life that many areas of our world are just not safe.

Two friends jog together on a regular basis and find this a great tension releaser. They are both at the same level of fitness so neither one is holding back or urging the other beyond her endurance level. As they are good friends, they can vent frustrations about other areas of their lives to each other during their jogs. It's a double whammy approach of getting exercise and exorcising some frustrations at the same time.

*Jog on, jog on
the footpath way.
– Shakespeare*

Walking has become known as one of the best exercises. Walking for health is being encouraged in fitness magazines. Mall walking clubs have sprung up. Living in a part of the country where winter walking is not always pleasant in the great outdoors, mall walking sounds like a good idea. However, whenever

*A walk for walk's sake.
– Paul Klee*

possible, I prefer the outdoors, especially the country. Nature can be healing, so, when possible, guide your walks near trees, flowers, water, grasses. Find some picturesque country roads that aren't too busy where the wildflowers have been left to grow rampantly along the verges. This treats both the eyes and the nose.

If you are seeking creative ideas, go out walking. Angels whisper to a man when he goes for a walk.
– Raymond Inmon

Swimming

Jonathan has been known to get up early every morning to swim a mile's worth of laps before going to work. He really enjoys this and finds it a great way to start his day. I don't think I could persuade my body to brave the cold water first thing in the morning

Tai chi

Tai chi consists of slow, precise, rhythmic movements which bring tranquillity. Tai chi is an exercise which is almost as relaxing to watch as it is to do. There are classes, television programs and books on this style of exercise.

I shall wear white flannel trousers, and walk upon the beach.
– T.S. Eliot

Yoga

Yoga slows you down, focusing your attention and breathing. There are often television programs explaining the techniques or classes given. I recommend giving them a try. I've also seen some good books and tapes on yoga.

My friend, John, began doing yoga after discovering the book *Yoga Over 40* in a secondhand bookstore. He finds he has more flexibility than ever. It's an exercise program he enjoys so he has stuck with it and actually misses it when he doesn't get a chance to do his regular session.

What are some exercises you do or would like to start doing? Feel free to jot them down in this space.

Fishing

It has been said that every hour spent fishing adds a day to your life. It can be one of the most relaxing sports there is. The last time I was fishing was during a summer when I was taking classes for a degree and working full time as well. My friends, Bob and John, and I had just completed a fairly heavy course. Bob suggested a day of canoeing and fishing as our reward for completing the course. A fabulous idea. The day turned out to be sunny and warm with a mild breeze. The lake was calm most of the day. We had a picnic lunch on the shore with the soft sound of the gentle waves as background music. Although only one fish was caught (and thrown back), the day was a total success.

Hiking

Hiking in the spring and fall are my favorites. The spring has such wonderful treasures waiting to be discovered: crocus, shooting stars, the fresh "spring-green" of the leaf buds. Fall has its glorious colors and scents. The air is just that little bit brisker and bracing. Hiking isn't just for the mountains. You can hike along a rolling country road or a riverbank.

Do be careful when you hike. Ensure you have comfortable clothing and shoes. If you are hiking in the woods, be aware of fire hazards and bear warnings for the area. If it's tick season, be sure to wear a hat and pull your socks over top of your pantlegs.

The fellowship of country roads is a goodly one, and in that fellowship one can find lifelong comrades, passing acquaintances, and a wisdom that can be gained, perhaps, in no other way. It is the wisdom of the fields and woods, compounded by the observing eye and the understanding heart; and it is a wisdom that does not grow old, that lasts until a man's hiking days are done, and then it brightens many a fireside hour.
– Arthur Wallace Peach

Playing

Playing is a wonderful relaxer. Have you ever watched children having a great time on the playground? Listened to their laughter and squeals of pure delight? Playing can bring back some of those feelings for you.

Our true age can be determined by the ways in which we allow ourselves to play.
– Louise Walsh

It's okay to be childlike (as opposed to being childish!). One of the first dates Jonathan and I went on was to the park to blow bubbles. From there we went to the swings where we "tickled our tummies." It was a wonderful spring day with the geese flying back home overhead and fluffy white clouds playing tag with the sun. You don't need a child with you for these activities, although you may feel more comfortable if you bring a "token" child along. And the child will certainly enjoy the outing as well. If you do take a child, slow down or speed up to his or her pace. Notice what interests the child. Regain that sense of wonder at the world.

Fly a Kite

Flying is largely a matter of having the right outlook.
– E.B. White

Either make or buy yourself a colorful kite. Then go out to a clear field and watch it soar. One day when Jonathan and I were out for a spring walk we happened upon a kite club. The kites were absolutely fantastic with long streamers of every color imaginable. The sky was awash with vibrant blues, reds, greens and yellows – a welcome splash of color after a long, drab winter.

Juggling

This requires concentration and a great sense of humor while you are learning it. I'm still trying to get my left hand to pass the bag with a sense of dignity to my right hand. My patience has improved greatly since attempting to learn this skill. I have also sat down on the floor in a heap of laughter at my antics. I must admit, I haven't been quite brave enough to entertain anyone with this display, but if laughter is the best medicine then I'm sure my juggling could cure a thousand ills.

As lookers-on feel
most delight,
That least perceive a
juggler's sleight,
And still the less they
understand,
The more th'admire his
sleight of hand.
– Samuel Butler

What are some play activities that you would like to try or try again?

Singing

Singing is a measure of ease and contentment for many people. Singing in the shower or humming while doing dishes lets everyone around know you're feeling okay about yourself and life in general. Belting out a song, filling in any spots where you don't remember the words, can express happiness.

Sing away sorrow, cast away care.
– Cervantes

Of course, sometimes you will also sing sad songs because that is the mood that suits you. Either way, it's a form of self-expression.

I celebrate myself, and sing myself.
–Walt Whitman

If you enjoy singing, you could look for a choir to join. This requires a certain amount of commitment, so be aware of your time constraints before heading into it.

If you can walk you can dance.
If you can talk you can sing.
– Zimbabwe saying

Find some song books of camp songs, goofy songs, folk tunes, popular songs and sing away. It's great fun.

Sports

You never really lose until you stop trying.
– Mike Ditka

Sports are a great way to get exercise and spend time with people. If you enjoy competition, then sports may be the way for you to release some tension.

Golf

I have never tried golf. It is on my list of "things to try before I die." Numerous friends are avid golfers. It would seem that it becomes somewhat addictive if these friends are anything to go by. They do enjoy it. From the cartoons you see with golf clubs wrapped around trees, I'm not totally sure this is a relaxing sport. However, as my friend Isobel says, "I'll get up eagerly at 5:30 on a Saturday morning to play golf. I can't say I'd do the same for housework."

My friend Maisie says for her it's not so much the game itself, as it is the chance to walk with friends in a pleasant setting. That definitely sounds relaxing.

In golf, as in life, the attempt to do something in one stroke that needs two is apt to result in taking three.
– Larry Wilde

Horseback Riding

I adore horseback riding. There is a certain thrill which accompanies the sight of riders galloping along a grassy verge or a beach. Swinging up onto this big animal, hearing the squeak of leather and the clop of the horse's hooves is a wonderful feeling. As long as the horse consents to just walking, I'm in heaven. If the horse even thinks about moving faster, a little bubble of panic grows ever so slowly. Needless to say, this is

There is no secret so close as that between a rider and his horse.
– Robert Smith Surtees

There are no handles to a horse, but the 1910 model has a string at each side of its face for turning its head when there is anything you want it to see.
– Stephen Leacock

not stress reducing. My friend Ann says I should go for the laziest horse!

My friend Lorraine, on the other hand, adores horses and has been riding forever. She can control just about any equine and finds great relaxation in grooming and riding them.

So, since I still love horses and riding, I watch it instead. There is a bit of longing which accompanies this but a great deal of enjoyment as well.

Skating

In skating over thin ice, our safety is in our speed.
– Ralph Waldo Emerson

Skating can be wonderfully relaxing – especially once you are past the stage where you spend a lot of the time sitting down suddenly! Somehow music helps you skate more rhythmically which, in turn, helps your balance. Ice skating has the added benefit of giving you lovely rosy cheeks. I mean the ones on your face, not the ones you keep plopping down on! They are more likely to be black and blue!

Skiing

Whether this is cross-country or downhill, getting out into the winter sunshine and brisk air does something for one's soul. It somehow seems as though exercising takes on a special meaning when you are also "braving the elements." Skiers are a friendly bunch, too. It's rare that a fellow cross-country skier will pass on the path without a friendly greeting and warm smile.

In winter, it can be more important than ever to get outside when the sun is shining. We tend to spend so much time inside when it's cold. Also, with the days being shorter, we seem to go to work in the dark and come home in the dark. This lack of sunshine can be depressing and stressful. So, get out in that winter sunshine whenever possible.

Tennis/Handball
Badminton/Squash

Jonathan and a friend play squash about once a week. They release some energy and tensions and have a friendly rivalry. They are at about the same level of play so it's a toss-up as to who will win each week. I think this helps to make the games more enjoyable.

Team Sports

A group from work get together in the early morning to play friendly hockey during the fall and winter. They are in it for the fun and exercise, although winning is also enjoyable.

You're gonna lose some ballgames and you're gonna win some ballgames and that's about it.
— Sparky Anderson

Note: Make sure that your teams are at similar levels of competitiveness and ability.

Volleyball

The need to win is the quietest of all impulses, an echo, yet it teases, pokes urgently in deepest corners. You think you don't care if you win or lose, that you've moved beyond that, but you do care, you do.
— Joan Clark

This used to be my favorite sport in high school. As an adult, I would get together with a friend and her church group to play once a week. It started out as a friendly get-together. If one team seemed to have a preponderance of good players, the teams were switched about to make them more even. This went on for a year or so. Then for some reason, it seemed that the need to win became stronger and stronger for some of the players. The ball was spiked more and more frequently. People were getting hurt. So, I decided this was no longer fun for me and dropped out.

Be aware that no matter what you choose as a stress-reducing activity, as soon as it no longer reduces your stress, it is your perfect right to stop doing it and find something else. This is not always easy to do, especially if a friendship is involved. In the long run, though, it is best.

What are some team sports in which you would like to become involved?

Travel

Travel doesn't need to be an exotic island to be relaxing. Sometimes all it takes is exploring a street you've never been down before. A friend of mine is "doing" her home town this summer because she's never been to the tourist attractions there.

Travel can be for many reasons – to visit family and friends, to explore new lands, to learn about another culture, to "get away from it all." You can travel alone, with friends or with a group of strangers who eventually become friends.

If you are traveling with someone, establish what each of your priorities are. If you want to relax on the beach with a book for three of the five days and your companion wants to see everything there is to see, then work it that you split up or compromise. Doing this well in advance of arrival saves a lot of tension.

Travel can also be in your mind. (This isn't too activating but it may give you an idea for your next active travels.) Sit back, relax, breathe deeply. Once you are in a state of relaxation, visualize that special place. Put yourself there. Be as wild and extravagant as you want to be.

We are all travellers in time. Our travels are always into the future. Each of us must make our own map of the best paths to take.
– Dan L. Costley and Ralph Todd

O travel light; as light That is, as a man can travel who will Still carry his body around because Of its sentimental value.
– Christopher Fry

Travel, in the younger sort, is a part of education; in the elder, a part of experience.
– Francis Bacon

I love to visualize a place with a hammock strung up between two palms. It's shady on the hammock but the day is sunny and warm. There is a brook softly bubbling away to itself as it makes its way to the nearby ocean. The sound of the waves is soothing. I have my books, my fresh fruit drink and an invisible shield which prevents bugs from getting near me except for the occasional brightly colored butterfly. I have played with this visualization so frequently I can get there in almost no time at all. That's the beauty of practicing relaxation techniques – they start to become second nature to you. They are there when you need them – and even when you just want them.

What other Activating ideas for relieving stress do you have?

Create

To create is to boggle the mind and alter the mood.
Once the urge has surged, it maintains its own momentum.
We may go along for the ride,
but when we attempt
to steer the course,
the momentum dies.
– Sue Atchley Ebaugh

Create

In this section you will find ideas to give outlet to your creative juices. Everyone is creative. Putting together a meal, imagining the characters as you read a book, folding a piece of paper into an airplane, or seeing lambs in the clouds are all creative acts. Creating truly relieves stress.

Our creative acts bring us satisfaction, enrich and stabilize our lives, enable us to express our own uniqueness, and clarify our flashes of insight into our complex existence.
– Gabriele Lusser Rico

Crafts

Being able to indulge myself in a variety of crafts is one of the great joys in my life. With all the crafts out there, there is bound to be one that is right for you – maybe even three or four or more.

Calligraphy

This is a soothing and relaxing personal hobby. It joins three of my passions – lettering, interesting sayings and gift giving. It's fun to find a saying just right for someone and then to use calligraphy to write it out for them on a blank card or some parchment paper. Receiving this sort of mail out of the blue is wonderful. Try creating your own alphabet style and use it to write letters or to design homemade cards.

Every artist was first an amateur.
– Ralph Waldo Emerson

Crochet

I went through a spell of crochet mania. I crocheted afghans and sweaters of all sorts for friends and relations. I prefer it to knitting because I can see the results faster. The patterns are becoming more sophisticated these days as well. I found an absolutely stunning book in the library called *The Crochet Sweater Book* by Sylvia Cosh. It has gorgeous patterns as well as information on yarns, textures and colors. Putting something together in beautiful colors can be exceedingly relaxing and rewarding.

Embroidery

This includes tapestry, crewel, cross-stitch and other related crafts. Watch as your work comes alive. My cousin, Elinor, lovingly worked for years on a glorious tapestry. It was a day of rejoicing and admiration when it was completed.

One Christmas, Sheena and I gave Mum and Dad a large red tablecloth with a poinsettia design to be cross stitched. A small section was started for Mum, the rest she did throughout the year. By the next Christmas and every year after, we use this beautiful cloth on the table for the Christmas meal. A new tradition has begun.

Had I the heavens' embroidered cloths,
Enwrought with gold and silver light,
The blue and the dim and the dark cloths
Of night and light and half light, . . .
– W. B. Yeats

Knitting

Sheena and Mum are great knitters.
They can look at a couple of patterns
and combine them to create a look all
their own.

A few years ago, Sheena took a photo-
graph she had snapped during a visit to
the west coast of British Columbia and
created a scenic sweater for me. It's
quite a thrill walking around in a piece
of art. They are both so accomplished at
knitting that they can sit and watch television or hold an intelligent conversation at the same time. Sheena says that
sometimes she feels guilty if she just
watches television. By knitting at the
same time, she feels as though she is ac-
complishing something.

Pottery

I discovered pottery and wheel throw-
ing about two years ago – a combination of exhilaration and frustration. The
frustration comes when that piece of
clay just won't get centred on the wheel.
The exhilaration is when the pot takes
shape before your eyes. It is a technique
I am still learning. It is great fun, especially if you don't mind getting dirty.

Sewing

Sewing is such fun! A couple of years ago I had a wonderful time making Halloween costumes for Jonathan and myself. There were some moments of tension when the machine broke down three times in a row. On the plus side, it did help me to practice my assertiveness as I kept lugging the recalcitrant machine back to the repair shop.

This year I have played with valances and pillow shams. I must admit that I "preen" a little whenever someone admires the valances. Even long after the actual activity of sewing is completed, there is still pleasure to be derived.

Sewing stuffed dolls or animals for children you know or for hospitals can give you and the children a wonderful warm glow. Ditto for making clothing for the needy.

Why not try creating a costume for Halloween this year? Then have a costume party. Look through the craft books and magazines in your local library. They are sure to spark some ideas.

Stained Glass

Jonathan has taken a couple of courses in stained glass. The results of his efforts are a Tiffany lamp which glows with warmth on a winter's evening and a clear and frosted beveled glass window hanging which would rival any you might find in a shop. He has plans for some larger pieces when time permits. It is a very precise hobby, requiring much planning and concentration; this helps to focus the mind.

Woodworking

Building something out of wood seems to me a glorious talent. It's been my father's hobby and I think his escape from tension for years. The smell of worked wood is wonderful. The actual coming together of useful pieces of furniture or candlesticks or toys must be a great feeling.

Move along these shades
In gentleness of heart;
with gentle hand
Touch – for there is a spirit
in the woods.
– William Wordsworth

My sister Sheena took a furniture building course one year. She has a pressured job which requires major stress-reducing techniques. Her course did a few things for her – it got her out of the house and thus away from the chores there as well as any "homework;" it let her create with her hands and head which she loves doing and is so very good at; and it introduced her to new people and ideas. The blanket chest which she built is a stunning addition to her living room decor.

What are some crafts you would like to learn or start doing again?

Creative Expression

This is where you can let yourself go creatively. The rules are few. You let the spirit move you. As you allow this style of creativity to flow through you, you will notice that stresses subside.

Designing

Designing is one of the activities with which I have the most fun. My friend, Colleen, has a niece who does wonderful things with blank paper and rubber stamps. It's always a delight to receive a wee note from Colleen to see what combination her niece has put together this time.

Lynne designs her own cards using photographs as well as her artistic talent. It is somehow very special to receive a

birthday card from Lynne which you
know was designed with you in mind.

Often, designing takes place all in the
mind. For example, picture yourself
stranded on a deserted tropical island
just like the Swiss family Robinson.
Now imagine the "home" you would
build for yourself and whomever you
decide is with you. Would it be at
ground level, underground, in a cave,
on a hill, up a tree, near water? Would it
be one big room or have partitions?
What materials would you use? How
would you defend it against wild animals? Would you have a garden? What
about recreation? Would there be slides,
swings? Designing in your mind has the
advantage of instant renovations with
none of the fuss and muss of real renovations.

Doodling

Doodling is a universal art form. Doodling isn't just for paper and pencil. It
can also be musical. Sometimes when
I'm in the shower, I will play with
sounds and notes. It's interesting to
hear how they combine and mix or not
mix. I also doodle with words – otherwise known as "making them up." For
example,"prossible" is a combination of
probable and possible. It's not one or
the other; it's sort of in-between.

Drawing

Some of my "best" drawings are when I look closely at familiar objects. For example, I did a great drawing of a single blade of grass one afternoon when I was studying. It helped to focus my mind so that when I went back to the books, I could actually understand what I was reading.

Drawing is the true test of art.
– J. A. D. Ingres

A useful activity when I'm angry is scribbling. I get out the colors I'm not that fond of and just go at it. I'll grit my teeth and bear down on the crayon or pencil crayon to help release the anger through my hand onto the paper. Usually it ends up just as scribbles but occasionally words or pictures start to form. Either way, the anger is dissipated onto the paper and out of me.

In an opposite vein, you could draw a fun picture using your favorite colors. Why not try using scented markers for this? Or get a children's coloring book and color in outrageous colors. Make the sky purple with green clouds if you wish.

Painting

To paint well is simply this: to put the right color in the right place.
– Paul Klee

Painting is something I play at without feeling particularly accomplished about.

A course I took in watercolors began
with the idea of having fun with it. I
used to go to courses with the idea that I
had to create something gorgeous by
the end of the second class! Now I go
with the idea that I am going to learn as
much as I can and have as much fun as
possible in the process. If I create anything worthwhile, it is a bonus. Taking
classes is much more relaxing with this
attitude. Besides, what one person
thinks is beautiful may not be what anyone else thinks is beautiful. That's okay.
If it pleases you then it serves a purpose. If it pleases someone else as well,
wonderful.

**What are some of your favorite ways to
express yourself creatively?**

Garden

Gardening is a lot of work and should
possibly have been included in the chapter, "Activate." However, it is much
more than hoeing, planting and weed-

*Gardening is an
instrument of
grace.*
– May Sarton

ing. It is planning, experimenting and being outdoors. It's being close to the earth and reaping the rewards.

Catalogues

The advantage of seed catalogues is that you can plan your garden in the middle of winter. Looking at the gorgeous pictures of flowers, fruits and vegetables also helps remind you that spring will come.

Angry I strode home
But stooping in
My garden
Calm old willow tree
– Ryota

Flowers

Arranging fresh flowers is a relaxing way to enjoy your garden. The wonder of flowers is their unique shapes, colors and scents. Looking in flower books to find the meanings of various flowers is an interesting pastime. "Lavender" can mean mistrust, which seems rather unfavorable until you read that asps liked to nest in the base of the lavender plant; then it makes more sense.

Buttercups and daisies,
Oh, the pretty flowers;
Coming ere the Springtime,
To tell of sunny hours.
– Mary Howitt

Indoor and Outdoor Gardens

In my opinion, house plants give life to a home. There is the added bonus that they help to purify the air. Real plants take some care, but they can be relaxing.

My parents live on Vancouver Island and garden almost all year long. They

What a man needs
in gardening is a
cast-iron back,
with a hinge in it.
– Charles D. Warner

have fruit trees as well as a vegetable
patch and flower gardens.

Memories

Memories of good times and special moments can help ease tensions on those
"bad" days.

*Memory is the power to
gather roses in winter.*
– Unknown

Memory Box

My memory box is a wonderful relaxer.
I keep all sorts of items in it such as
booklets from plays or museums, a letter from a friend written on birchbark
and a plastic necklace of blue hearts
from a New Year's cracker. The box itself is rather tattered and worn, so I am
on the lookout for a pretty new box or
wrapping paper for a plain box. In some
ways I hate to give up the original box
as it is now part of the memories. Memory boxes can be cigar boxes or pretty
colored boxes which hold larger items
that just don't make it into a scrapbook.

*Memory is the treasury
and guardian
of all things.*
– Cicero

Scrapbook

Remember scrapbooks from when you
were a kid in school? You would paste
in reports, creative writing assignments,
cards from your friends, notes from the
teacher. If you are sentimental, then
keep one of your daily life now. The
ticket stub from that fabulous play, a

Oft, in the stilly night,
Ere Slumber's Chain has bound me,
Fond Memory brings the light Of other days around me.
– Thomas Moore

A thousand fantasies begin to throng into my memory . . .
– John Milton

special card from a loved one, a good Chinese fortune, a card that you just fell in love with at the card shop and couldn't bear to part with, a single rose pressed from a Valentine's bouquet, photos of the picnic on the hill. I find scrapbooks more fun than photo albums because I can write next to the photos and other items. It helps keep the memory more accurate.

When my sister and I were small, Mum kept the new baby, birthday and Christmas cards which we received. When we were old enough, she helped us to put them into scrapbooks. It's interesting to look back on these as a record of our childhoods. It's also interesting to look through them as a mini history of cards.

What are some of your favorite memories?

Mind Mapping

Mind mapping, or idea mapping, is a technique for personal brainstorming. It allows you to be freewheeling with your ideas and connections. For example, if you are planning a party, you can idea map the various elements so that you remember to get everything ready.

I use mind mapping for my "to do" list at work and on weekends. I got the idea from Joyce Wycoff's book, *Mindmapping*. In the centre of the page, I write the span of the week. From there, I web and connect all the things that I feel I'd like to accomplish for the week. Along the side of the page I write each day's date. As the day comes up, I highlight the items that I want to do that day in yellow. When an item is completed, I go over the yellow highlight with blue, which changes the color to green. As I look at my list I can tell at a quick glance what has been done – anything in green. I can also see what is left and carry things over to the next day.

Photography

Photography has such potential for creativity and relaxation. I especially enjoy taking photos of nature. The beauty is ever-changing.

. . . in adventure and in photography, as in life, being in the right place at the right time can sometimes mean everything.
– J. A. Kaulis

Enter contests. Label and organize your photos. Throw out the duds. Enjoy your photos. Share them. (Not all 2 000 of your trip to Mexico at once!) Send labeled copies to friends and relatives. Make mini scrapbooks for friends and/or relatives of their visits with you or of special moments in your life.

Theatre

Theatre is irresistible; organize the theatre.
– Matthew Arnold

In cities, there are usually a number of amateur theatre groups about that will be delighted to have you with them in the capacity of set designer, actor/actress, ticket sales, costume designer, etc. It's great fun and can be a good release. Be prepared to pitch in and help with just about anything. If you are shy, try some behind the scenes work. Whatever you decide to try, have fun with it.

You might want to try mime or clowning as well. I've been fascinated by miming for ages. It's incredible how simple body movements can "speak" so loudly.

Writing

Better to write for yourself and have no public, than to write for the public and have no self.
– Cyril Connolly

Writing can be a great stress reliever. Writing has many avenues, from expressing exactly what is bothering you or moving into the realm of fantasy, to writing about the happiness in your life.

This can take the form of a journal or
diary or be jotted down in a notebook
you carry with you, or even entered into
a computer.

Blessings Book

One of the nicest things I have ever
done for myself is keeping a "Blessings
Book," a small blank book beside the
bed, in which I list my blessings. It's a
wonderful book to pick up and peruse
when you're starting to feel a bit down.
It is an ongoing book which will hope-
fully never be completed.

*And twenty minutes
more or less
It seemed so great my
happiness,
That I was blessed and
could bless.
– W. B. Yeats*

It lists items such as peach clouds at sunset, big fat snowflakes drifting silently
and slowly from a slate gray sky, purring kittens, hugs, dew sparkling like dia-
monds in the morning light, bubble
gum, root beer flavored jelly beans, fire-
places, turkey sandwiches with dressing
and cranberry sauce, the scent of roses,
Jonathan's smile, books. Sometimes I
illustrate a blessing.

The Blessings Book is a favorite book
for reading and writing in. This is also a
book you may enjoy sharing.

Book/Story

Have an idea for a book? Why not go
ahead and start writing it? It doesn't

have to be the greatest novel of all time. You may decide that it is only for you. Or you may decide, like A.A. Milne, to write stories for the child in your life. Go ahead and do it. It's your life and they are your stories.

Not that the story need be long, but it will take a long while to make it short.
– Henry David Thoreau

There are numerous creative writing classes around. There are also books available to help you start writing. Some of these are listed in the Sources section.

Journal

Journals are wonderful. I keep one or two going all the time. I used to try to write in them every night. I still aim for that, but no longer get upset with myself if I don't do it. After all, it's my choice. For me, the best things about journals are that you can release a lot of grief into them and then walk away from it. I also find that by taking the time to write about a problem, I also take the time to really think about it. Things seem to fall into place when I write about them. Another great thing about journals is that they are very interesting to read years later.

A journal is a place to explore all the little happinesses and large joys of your unique life. A place to have fun!
– Jean Bryant

For instance, one day I started thinking about abuse. I picked up my notebook and wrote about functional and dysfunctional scars, how one can be scarred by an event but still function. The functional scar reminds you of the event but doesn't prevent you from moving on with your life. The dysfunctional scar not only reminds you of the event but also restricts your movements.

These random thoughts used to be lost into the air. By writing your thoughts down, you will keep them for thinking about again and again.

Record each day in some way: The lessons you learn. The good that you do. The good that happens to you. The insights you have. Anything else that seems of interest.
–John-Roger and Peter McWilliams

Note

Leaving a note for a loved one is a way to say you care. Pop it on the hall mirror or into a briefcase or lunch box for a pleasant surprise at work or school. It can be anything from a cute joke to an inspiring saying to a few words of encouragement to "I love you." Not only does this please the recipient, but it gives you a warm glow knowing that it will brighten someone's day. Remember that you can be the loved one for whom the note is intended. Write a few for yourself and scatter them around in pant pockets, dresser drawers, etc. They will be fun to rediscover.

Poem

Poetry has long been underrated by many. It can have a soul and wisdom and wit all its own. It comes from your innermost depths. When you write your poetry, have fun with it.

A favorite type of expression for me is the "word association" poem. These are fun and easy and can tell you a lot about how you are feeling. Start with a word and then just keep adding other words and phrases to it as you think of them. Sheena did one for me for one of my birthdays. She put it on large white posterboard and added dried flowers, drawings and pictures from magazines. It was a wonderful birthday card which I moved around with me for years until time wore it out. (Regretfully, when I finally threw it out prior to yet another move, I was in such haste that I neglected to write down the poem.)

Here is a sample of an associated random thoughts poem based on the word "sunshine."

A poem should not mean,
But be.
– Archibald Macleish

Sunshine

dapples through leafy branches

shadow figures on the ground

cloud forms moving along the fields

chasing

smiles

chubby cheeks

friends

warmth

glowing embers

twilight

Tiny Book

Create a tiny book for someone who is feeling low or sad, sick with the flu or about to embark on a great adventure. Fill it with appropriate sayings, memories of times together, hilarious jokes or puns, maybe even a brainteaser or two.

Make a personalized book for someone. It lets them know they are special. One Christmas, Jonathan asked for an art book. Feeling in a mischievous mood at the time, I decided to make him an "Art's Book." My friend Jackie helped me to come up with an idea for each letter of the alphabet. It was great fun to research, create and draw this mini book. For example, "B" was for Boticelli. The drawing was a caricature of a portion of a famous Boticelli painting. Jonathan thought it was a hoot.

Make a personalized book for yourself. Let yourself know that you think you are special.

QUEEN MARGARET COLLEGE LIBRARY

Writing is both restful and frustrating. When it comes together, it is a fabulous experience. When the words won't come out, it is torture. On days when nothing comes out the way I want it to, I just continue to put the thoughts down in their garbled manner anyway. I know that if I just get them down, I can work on them again another day when things do make sense. Amazingly, some days when I feel as though everything is a jumbled mess, I'll look back at what I've written days later and wonder why I thought it was garbled. Writing is a very personal experience. When you write to relieve stress, write for you.

What are some of your creative activities for relieving stress?

Surround

When the objects we use every day
and the surroundings we live in
have become in themselves a work of art then we will be
able to say that we have achieved a balanced life style.
– *Bruno Munari*

Surround

This section deals with what is around you. If you are not comfortable either physically or emotionally with your environment, try making some changes. It could be as simple as pinning an attractive postcard onto the wall or as involved as redecorating an entire room.

All people are builders, creators, molders, and shapers of the environment; we are the environment.
– Robert Sommer

Beauty

Whenever possible, use attractive mugs, pens, pencils, plates, place mats, blankets, sheets, towels – things that make you feel good. Create beauty in your environment with simple items like a gorgeous postcard on your bulletin board, an interesting piece of pottery to hold the pens by the phone or a beautiful plant on your desk.

Gazing on beautiful things acts on my soul, which thirsts for heavenly light.
– Michelangelo

Ceremony

Use a favorite mug for your morning tea or coffee. Sit down with it and enjoy the aroma, flavor and warmth of the liquid, the feel and look of the mug or cup. Use a goblet for that water to perk yourself up and remind yourself you are special and deserving. A slice of lemon in a glass water jug "sweetens" the water and looks elegant.

Home is where we return for fulfillment and wholeness.
– Alexandra Stoddard

Ritual is the technique of giving life.
– Thomas J. Peters & Robert H. Waterman, Jr.

Put that hot dog and coleslaw on a china plate and eat by candlelight with soft music in the background. Sound a bit pretentious? Maybe. But give it a try. You may just find a new ritual for hot dogs!

Colors

Use a variety of colors in order to keep human responses continually active and to avoid visual adaptation or emotional monotony.
– Faber Birren

Colors can do a lot for your environment. If you live or work in a place where the colors just are not you, see what you can do to change them. You may not be allowed to paint the walls, so you will have to be creative. Pillows, afghans, large posters and pictures to cover a LOT of the wall can help.

And life is color and warmth and light
And a striving evermore for these;…
– Julian Grenfell

The warm colors (reds, oranges, yellows and yellow-greens) are considered to be stimulating. The cool colors (blues, violets, purples and blue-greens) are considered to be relaxing. Too much of any color can be distressing. For example, a red room can be invigorating to begin with but if you stay in too long, you can become irritable or exhausted. A bland off-white room can become boring without color accents.

The purest and most thoughtful minds are those which love color the most.
– Ruskin

**What colors soothe you? Which ones
enliven you?**

Dressing

You may be wondering why "Dressing"
is in the section "Surround." Well, you
are part of the environment. How you
dress will affect how you feel as well as
how those around you feel.

Your style of dress says a lot about how
you feel about yourself. It speaks of
your comfort level with yourself and
with the tasks of the day.

*Comfort is perhaps the
ultimate luxury.
– Billy Baldwin*

Don't forget about color when you are
dressing. Choose and use colors that
look good on you and make you feel
good. I have tried to have basic color
themes in my wardrobe throughout the
years but find that I enjoy too many colors to limit them to a few.

If you aren't sure which colors suit you, ask a trusted friend to go shopping with you. You don't have to buy anything, just try on outfits of different colors. If possible, try the same outfit in different colors. Or, you could have your colors done by a reputable specialist.

If you are going to an interview, dress appropriately. Above all, have clean, neatly pressed clothes. This will help give you confidence. I read once that blue is the best color to wear to an interview in North America. Apparently, it is a favored color. It is thought to project values of truth, accomplishment and serenity. Not bad values to be projecting at an interview!

On those days when I am doing something with which I'm not comfortable, I dress exceptionally well to help boost my confidence. I'll wear a favorite outfit in an uplifting color.

Which are your favorite outfits? What is it about them that makes them favorites?

Home Decorating

I thoroughly enjoy looking at display
homes, decorating magazines and
friends' homes. There are always one or
two ideas there for the taking. Take the
time to really look. Assess how various
styles make you feel. Do you like the
feel of the sophistication of the modern
style? Is that you? How about the country style? The romantic? Maybe you like
a few different styles. You could enjoy
an eclectic home. Or you could try different styles for different rooms.

Since we spend so much of our days at
work, we shouldn't forget to decorate
our workplace as well. A special photo-
graph or art print near the desk can help
brighten an area.

*Note: First, check that office rules allow
this.*

*Whatever serves to
heighten the enjoyment
of home, and add fresh
graces to the domestic
hearth, must be worthy
of encouragement and
culture.
– Shirley Hibberd*

Pictures

Collect postcards, greeting cards, pictures from magazines, posters, photographs, wrapping paper and pictures.
Try various arrangements for them.
Sometimes you might want just one or
two scattered about. At other times you
might want to try a collage effect.
Change them as the mood hits you.

*Pictures are consolers of
loneliness; they are a
sweet flattery to the soul;
they are a relief to the
jaded mind; they are win-
dows to the imprisoned
thought; they are books;
they are histories and ser-
mons – which we can
read without the trouble
of turning over the leaves.
– Henry T. Tuckerman*

You can use small picture stands for postcards, photos and favorite greeting cards. Frames come in all shapes and sizes these days as well as a variety of prices. Change the matting used around the picture to see what effect you can make. Decorate the matting with bright or pastel colors.

If you have a bulletin board, try painting the frame your favorite color and covering the cork part with material that picks up the frame's color.

Style

I have a binder with pictures that I like from magazines. They range from chairs that I find interesting and cozy-looking dens to bedding sheet designs. There is also a section on colors which have caught my eye in magazines and at paint stores. When I look through this binder, I can see what it is I want for my home. It gives me a goal. Before I started doing this, I really had no idea what my style was. I knew what I didn't like but wasn't so sure of what I did like. The idea came from Alexandra Stoddard's *Daring to Be Yourself.* You can keep a scrapbook, binder or file folders for different rooms, clothing, gardens, dishes, even a list of book titles which you would like to read. It's an in-

Nothing adds more to the warmth and personality of a room than objects you love.
– Billy Baldwin

When we see a natural style we are quite surprised and delighted . . .
– Blaise Pascal

teresting way to discover who you are
and what your tastes are.

What styles help to relax you?

Housework

Really! I haven't gone too far. House-
cleaning can be relaxing. First, put on
some spirited music and see how much
easier it is to wash that floor or dust that
bookcase. Make up games as you clean,
contests with yourself. Can I get these
dishes washed before three tunes have
completed? Or use the cleaning time as
thinking time. After all, how much
thinking about the actual cleaning job
do you have to do? Take pride in a job
well done. Keeping your home or work
space clean and neat sends out a message that you care.

*Nothing is so fatiguing as
the eternal hanging on of
an uncompleted task.
– Henry James*

Household Chore

Take your least favorite chore – the one
you consistently keep putting off hop-

*Every kind of work can be a
pleasure. Even simple
household tasks can be an
opportunity to exercise and
expand our caring,
our effectiveness,
our responsiveness.*
– *Tarthang Tulku*

*Perhaps the most valuable
result of all education is the
ability to make yourself do
the thing you have to do
when it has to be done,
whether you like it or not.*
– *Aldous Huxley*

ing that the "cleaning gnomes" will
drop by and do it for you – and set up a
schedule. You will do it once a day,
twice a week, once a month. Also, set
up a reward system. For example, you
get to rent that movie or eat that chocolate bar if you manage to keep to your
schedule. If you don't keep to the schedule, decide to try harder next week.
Don't fuss at yourself. After all, the
world didn't come to an end.

When you are in a situation where you
share tasks with others, there is a higher
possibility of stresses arising. Be aware
that different people have different
schedules and different quality control
levels. It used to bother me greatly as a
child when I was interrupted from what
I was enjoying in order to complete a
chore on someone else's time schedule.
(Of course, according to my time schedule, I probably felt that sometime before
the next ice age would be soon enough
for chores.) This enters into the realm of
personal relations and interactions,
which is not the scope of this book.
However, here are a few ideas for
shared tasks.

Occasionally switch tasks. Have training sessions for tasks. This is especially
important for children who may have
"seen" you do the task a hundred times
but never really paid attention. Give
time frames which allow the other per-

son(s) to have control over completion of the task. Discuss quality standards and make compromises when necessary. Help each other out when necessary. Don't let one person end up with all the "yuck" jobs.

A couple of interesting books on the subject of housework are *Speed Cleaning* and *Spring Cleaning*, both by Jeff Campbell and The Clean Team.

Light

I love light. The only time I attempt to block it is in the height of summer when the apartment becomes unbearably warm. Otherwise, the living room drapes are almost constantly open. Right now, the days are becoming noticeably shorter and it saddens me. The thought of getting up in the dark does not appeal to me. I much prefer to be awakened by the sunshine. I live in a climate where for about four months of the year I go to work in the dark, spend my day in a windowless office and then come home in the dark. Noon hour outings have great appeal during this time.

At work, my windowless cubicle is in a windowless open space. The main lighting is by fluorescent lights with an incandescent task light on my desk. Although it is not my favorite lighting, I

A single sunbeam is enough to drive away many shadows.
– St. Francis of Assisi

Nothing is more life-enhancing and joyful than natural light flooding your home. Natural light is energy and your life force.
– Alexandra Stoddard

have become more used to it. By removing some of the fluorescent bulbs, I have managed to make my space less "brilliant" in the cold white light sense and warmer by using the incandescent task lighting. There are things you can do with lighting to make your spaces appeal to you. Whenever possible, don't just complain about the situation, letting negative, stressful feelings build up – do something to change the situation.

What style of lighting relaxes you most? How can you incorporate that style into your environments?

Nature

How much do you like natural scenes? Can you incorporate them into your living and work spaces? A floral arrangement of fresh or dried flowers can do wonders for a room. Pictures of favorite scenes or places visited can give you a lift each time you look at them. Onto what do your windows face? If it's your yard, what can you do to enhance the view? If it's a brick wall or another building, how can you enhance the rest of the room to compensate for that?

Whenever possible, go to nature. Let the visual and auditory beauties of the natural world around you help to ease your stresses. This doesn't necessarily mean a trip to the mountains or the lake or the beach, although those are wonderful ideas. It can be as simple as going to a neighborhood park or even to your backyard and really looking at the trees, grass, flowers, dirt, garden, weeds and listening to the birds and squirrels.

Nature is the living, visible garment of God.
— Goethe

One day, I was quite nervous about an upcoming appointment, so went to the football stadium grounds across the street from my apartment. I sat in the shade of a tree and really looked at its bark for about five minutes. Suddenly, I started seeing all sorts of faces and expressions in the bark. I pulled out the only paper I had with me at the time (a paycheque stub) and began drawing the faces and thinking about tree spirits. It calmed me right down, so that I could look at the upcoming appointment rationally instead of from a base of nerves.

You can't be suspicious of a tree, or accuse a bird or squirrel of subversion or challenge the ideology of a violet.
— Hal Borland

Organizing

Organizing and planning can make a huge difference in stress levels. Once you get into the habit of organizing yourself and your space, you will find that you have extra time as well as more energy.

Planning

Keep yourself on track with planning in advance. Keep a calendar handy to jot down special dates for classes, dinners, anniversaries, birthdays, etc. Be sure to plan some breaks and time for yourself while you are jotting down your engagements. I'm serious about this! Actually write down in the calendar that on Saturday morning you will be unavailable until 11:30 or on Tuesday evening from 7:30 to 8:30 you are booked. If someone calls to book that time with you, say you are previously engaged. You are allowed to have time for you! But you may have to plan for it rather than take what is left over.

The purpose of learning to employ every minute properly is to unclutter our hours, deliver us from feverish activity and earn us true leisure.
– Robert R. Updegraff

Is your calendar so full that you get tired just looking at it? If this is the case, then look at only a small portion at a time. In the morning, check the full day's worth so you know what to wear or take for the day; after that break it down into smaller chunks. Use a high-lighter in a favorite color to highlight those things you enjoy doing. This gives you something to look forward to. You may want to use a special color for those times that are booked for yourself; times when you will be uninterrupted so you can relax or get at that job which requires your total concentration.

Who begins too much
accomplishes little.
– German Proverb

A time-saving trick that I use for ap-pointments is not just to write down the time and person's name, but also the phone number and/or address. Having this right in my day book has saved me a lot of time. If an appointment was made well in advance, I'll call to con-firm. It's easy with the phone number right there. If I haven't been to an ap-pointment location before, I try to drive by at an earlier time to gauge how long it will take to get there, to discern the best route and parking availability. I hate being late. To me, being late is stressful. I dislike feeling rushed, espe-cially when I'm driving. I also feel rude when I am late, as I know time is a pre-cious commodity for everyone.

What is this life, if
full of care,
We have no time to
stand and stare?
– W. H. Davies

Self

I am a list maker – groceries, "to do," party planning, book ideas, reading lists, Christmas lists, meal lists; if it can be listed, I've probably done it. Making

Time for a little something.
– A. A. Milne

*Mix a little foolishness
with your serious plans;
it's lovely to be silly at the
right moment.*
– Horace

lists helps me to remember to do things without having to keep it all in my head. It also helps to prioritize items in terms of time limits and/or importance. Once I began listing things, I found that I seemed to have extra time. Somehow, by organizing the activities on lists, I had unintentionally begun managing my time better.

Another technique which is a good memory aid is phone answering machines. It's all very well to make lists but if you forget to look at them or leave them at the office or at home they aren't too helpful. If I promise to bring something from home to someone, I immediately ask if I may use their phone. I call my home number and leave myself a reminder. That blinking light always catches my eye. As soon as I see the light or listen to the message, I do the task required.

You might want to try the technique of popping Post-it notes on mirrors, computers, doors, car dash, etc. Jot down what you want to remind yourself or someone else of on the note and stick it in a prominent position. At home and the office, have a special location for notes where everyone knows to look. A friend of mine carries a small size of Post-it notes with her always. She finds this works better for her than a small notebook.

Surroundings

This is a personal preference. To me, a disorganized space is stressful. I tend to have from three to seven projects on the go at all times, both at work and at home. If I didn't organize my environment, I probably wouldn't be able to walk through the door! I use a lot of labeled boxes and see-through plastic boxes for my projects. For example, all my Halloween stuff – costumes, decorations, party ideas, are in one box. Christmas decorations, cards and gift wrap are in another. Sewing supplies take up about four boxes. A quilt that I am working on is stored in a wicker basket. Even the books in my library are organized by topic so that I know where to look for things. The bed in the spare room is the one place that is total and utter chaos. It receives everything that is waiting to be organized, creating a mad panic when overnight guests arrive.

Being organized does not mean the same as being neat. Being organized means having a system – one that enables you to find what you need when you need it.
– Sonia Schlenger

For others, clutter is a way of life; as long as no one touches anything, they know exactly where everything is. Choose your own style and own method of organizing but do organize.

What are some things you can do to give yourself more time for those things you really enjoy doing?

Sound/Noise Levels

True silence is the rest of the mind; it is to the spirit what sleep is to the body, nourishment and refreshment.
– William Penn

Some days the noise drives you crazy. Other days it's the quiet that disturbs you. Have a set of soothing and activating sounds for each occasion. Children's recordings are great activators. I find musicals and folk dance music great for getting me out of the doldrums. When I need something more restful, I try classicals such as Pachelbel's Canon. A list of some favorite pieces for activating and soothing is given in the Sources section.

Take care of the sense, and the sounds will take care of themselves.
– Lewis Carroll

Some days you don't want any noise, not even soothing music. Might I suggest earplugs? Actually, if you live in the city, it is difficult to find a truly quiet spot. Try the library, art gallery, or study hall at the local college or university. There might be a tolerable low murmur.

My friend, Dan, says that the noise of city life really gets to him at times. He finds that taking a weekend trip to nature helps immensely. The songs of the birds, murmur of the wind in the trees and chortling of the water in a stony brook can soothe him like nothing else.

Sound-Deadening Techniques

If your home vibrates with sound, try some sound-deadening techniques such as putting up corkboard tiles on the walls or draping material from the ceiling to the floor. In my office/spare room, I hung sheers around the bed – the one that keeps receiving all the "to be organized" stuff. They not only help to muffle noises, they hide the "junk" as well as give the room an Arabian Nights feel. I also draped the filing cabinet and low chest of drawers with soft blue material. Runners of an abstract print which picks up the blue were added. The clatter of the keyboard is softened by all this material, making the room a nicer place to work.

In silence she reposes:
Ah! would that I did too.
– Matthew Arnold

Elected Silence, sing to me
And beat upon my whorled ear,
Pipe me to pasture still and be
The music that I care to hear.
– Gerard Manley Hopkins

White Noise

My upstairs neighbors have children who are frequently rambunctious when

I am trying to sleep. They also give piano lessons which have been known to drive me to distraction. My solution is to turn on a large floor fan which emits a nice steady hum. The hum blocks out the extraneous noises but soon floats into the background of my awareness. It certainly helps prevent me from becoming annoyed with my neighbors.

At work, my office space is in a landscaped office zone. That's the type that have freestanding short walls and no doors. Most of the time there's no problem working there. However, occasionally there are so many conversations going on around me that I just can't concentrate. When this happens, I generally pull out my Walkman and softly play a soothing classical piece. It's not enough to distract me from my task, but is enough to drown out the myriad of conversations occuring around me.

Stress-Free Zone

We need varying degrees of privacy for sharing secrets, planning ahead, looking back, day dreaming, cogitating, evaluating our lives – being creative.
– Joan Kron

Appoint an area of your home where you can relax without interruptions. When you are in this area, no one may bother you except in a dire emergency, like the cat has the cockatiel in his mouth and is preparing to add salt and pepper. It could be your spare room, a certain chair, a spot in the basement or even the bathroom (although emergencies might arise more often with this choice unless you have more than one bathroom). Take some time just "to be" when you are in this "zone." Resolutely refuse to worry about anything. Relax, regroup, give yourself a chance to breathe deeply.

Temperature

If you are too cold or too hot in your environment, then you are not comfortable; this is a stressor. Find techniques for adjusting the temperature. At the office, I am usually cold while others around are comfortable. An inexpensive space heater has solved that difficulty.

At home, whether I'm comfortable or hot or cold depends greatly on what I'm doing. It's rare that I'm hot. When I'm working at the computer, I frequently feel the cold start creeping up my legs and then the back of my neck tightens perceptibly. If I'm aware soon enough, I can throw an afghan over my lap or turn up the heat before it reaches the point of being uncomfortable. If I'm too engrossed in what I'm doing though, it frequently leads to cold legs, a sore neck and a headache. (Obviously I haven't trained myself yet to incorporate regular stretching into my computer time. I'm working on it though, by programming the silent alarm to flash at regular intervals. This reminds me to stretch and look into the distance for a short break.)

Toys

Lighten up your work space. It doesn't mean that you won't concentrate on your job. It means that you have a sense of fun. It can also help to heighten your creativity on the job if you take time out occasionally to play. It will also reduce your stress level.

Jackie, a friend at work, has a miniature basketball hoop on her wall and a Nerf basketball. Visitors to her office frequently take a few shots before leaving. She also has a suction dart "gun" which she uses to release some frustrations. Shooting harmless darts at deadline dates or recalcitrant projects is quite fun.

What are some things you could do for your environment to make it more pleasant?

Business should be fun. Without fun, people are left wearing emotional raincoats most of their working lives. Building fun into business is vital; it brings life into our daily being. Fun is a powerful motive for most of our activities and should be a direct path of our livelihood. We should not relegate it to something we buy after work with money we earn.
– Michael Phillips

I will make you brooches and toys for your delight Of bird-song at morning and star-shine at night.
– R. L. Stevenson

Learn

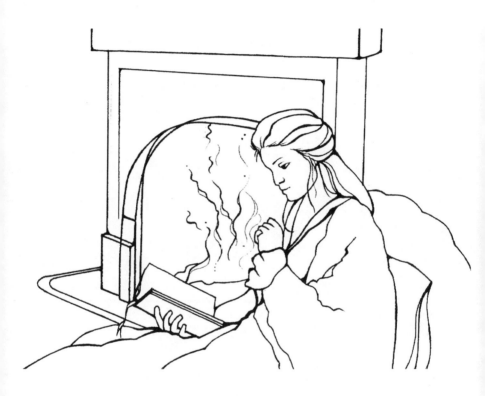

Still I am learning.
— Michelangelo

Learn

Learning does not stop when school is out. For that matter, learning did not start with school. Learning is continuous, ongoing, forever. The more you learn, the more control you have over yourself and the situations in which you find yourself.

I wish we could all retain the childlike curiosity we had in our youth when everything was a wonder to us. We wanted to know the why and how of everything.

What are some of the questions that pop into your head now? I think of things like how do birds in nesting colonies tell their chicks apart? When doctors shine that light in your ears, what are they looking for and at? Which came first, three-ring binders or three-hole punches? When it's -35°C for weeks on end, how do the winter birds keep warm? How do three-toed sloths ever get together to mate? When was the first pottery wheel used and who came up with the idea? How is it that some of us know from a very young age what we want to be when we grow up and others of us continue searching for large portions of our lives?

Life is for doing, learning, and enjoying.
– John-Roger & Peter McWilliams

Man can learn nothing except by going from the known to the unknown.
– Claude Bernard

If you want knowledge, you must take part in the practice of changing reality. If you want to know the taste of a pear, you must change the pear by eating it yourself.
– Mao Tse-tung

Try to retain your ability to question and wonder. It will help to keep you young.

Assertiveness

If you want to stay healthy and well-balanced, you need to set limits for yourself.
– Karen Caesar

Learn to say "no" when that is what you want to say. Develop your self-esteem and don't let anyone, not even yourself, take it away. There are numerous books and courses on assertiveness. When you develop assertiveness, stress is reduced because you are better able to handle those situations that used to frighten, fluster or annoy you. You can learn how to set limits for yourself; how to pull back from the emotions of situations so that the facts can be dealt with; how to create win/win situations and how to face problems as they arise rather than stewing over them for ages.

Every difficulty slurred over will be a ghost to disturb your repose later on.
– Chopin

Basic Home Maintenance

A house is a living machine.
– Le Corbusier

Learn what to do when something goes wrong. That way you won't need to panic right away. You may not even need to panic later! You will also learn when to call a professional and when you can handle it yourself.

Basic Mechanics

Learn how to keep the car in reasonable condition. Learn what those funny noises indicate and how to approach your mechanic with knowledge instead of blind trust. Talk with other car owners. Find out which garages or mechanics they recommend. Have a more knowledgeable friend listen to that strange noise. It may be as simple as a stone caught in the hubcap.

Books/Library

Books can open up vistas for you from party games to philosophy, from science to science fiction. I adore books. I adore the library that allows me to learn so much, meet new friends, discover new authors, and reintroduce myself to beloved old friends. I'm blessed with a love of reading for which I make time.

What are some books that help you relieve stress?

Be a reader. Read anything and everything, the more the better. Keep a book on the fire of your mind all the time. Follow your fancy. Read books you like. Then, for a change, read a book you don't like — you may stumble into a new world.
— Rudolph Flesch

Courses

I've been "going to school" since 1956, and every year since "graduating" I look at the classes available and sigh over the fact that I just don't have time to learn it all. I enjoy taking classes in the evenings and on weekends. Some of my friends take them over their lunch hours. My interests are wide, so I've taken everything from assertiveness training to pottery to cooking to Tai chi classes. Taking non-credit courses means that there is no pressure on you to pass an exam or write a great term paper. You can attend for the pure joy of learning.

Each opportunity to become more aware, more sensitive, and in effect more intelligent, brings out more of the inherent genius in each of us.
– Peter Kline

Computers

Learn how to use one. Learn a new program. Teach yourself a new aspect of a familiar program. Find a guru if need be. Above all, don't be afraid of them. They are just machines.

Anyone who stops learning is old, whether this happens at twenty or eighty. Anyone who keeps learning not only remains young, but becomes constantly more valuable regardless of physical capacity.
– Harvey Ullman

Cooking Lessons

I took some microwave cooking lessons once and was amazed at what I could actually do with my microwave beyond popping corn and reheating leftovers! Taking lessons can open whole new avenues in eating for you. The advantage of

There is always room for improvement – it's the biggest room in the house.
– Louise Heath Leber

cooking classes is that you get to learn shortcuts and interesting decorative ideas as well as the actual cooking techniques.

Try a class on gourmet, ethnic, or vegetarian cooking. Take a class on bread making or cake decorating. There are numerous options. Try them and bon appétit.

Craft Lessons

Have you long admired a certain craft technique? Why not try taking a class to learn how to do it yourself? Craft stores often give lessons or have notices about lessons.

Languages

Take a course and make new friends. Use tapes or records from the library. Being able to speak another language fluently or even in "tourist" mode is wonderful. Frequently, when you learn a new language you also get a taste of the country from which it comes. It's like getting bonus geography and sociology lessons wrapped up in the language.

Physical Activities

You may want to learn some sports. There are many places which offer courses in swimming, tennis, squash, basketball, etc. Try them. Not only will you learn a new sport or work on perfecting a favorite, you'll also get a stress-reducing workout and a chance to make some new friends.

Self-Help

When you begin to improve yourself, whether it be through learning to dress for success or practicing positive affirmations for better self-control, you can probably find a book or two on the subject. My advice is to borrow some from the local library to find out which styles suit you. Just as some diets may work for you while others don't, some self-help techniques will be more effective for you than others. You might also want to try different classes on the same subject to get differing points of view.

Stress Management

I recently attended a class on Stress Management for Women. Each time I take a class, I learn something new or a new way of putting something "old" together. Try a class on stress management. Read some books. There are stress management resources that are very specific, as well as more general resources.

Time Management

Time management is exciting. It's absolutely amazing how much more can be
accomplished, including finding time
for yourself, when you learn to manage
your time. For me, the main things in
time management are writing everything down so it's handy, learning to
say "no" and planning time for myself
to do the things I enjoy.

*You are the only one who
can steal your own time,
talent and
accomplishments.
— Denis Waitley*

Video & Photography

Take a class in using your home video
camera. Create some great memories to
be enjoyed again and again.

Learn how to take those fabulous photos. Learn how to make the most of
your camera.

Expand Your Horizons

Basically, what this section advocates is
that you keep expanding your horizons
whether that be through taking courses,
reading, talking with friends or thinking. The larger your comfort zone, the
more often you feel at ease, less stressed.

*A man is not idle because
he is absorbed in thought.
There is a visible labor and
there is an invisible labor.
— Victor Hugo*

You don't need to go far to expand your
horizons. Go to the library and scan the
magazines. Find some that you

wouldn't normally read and peek through them. Take a different route to the park or to the office or to your neighbor's back door.

Take a small child for a walk and let him or her take the lead. Go where they go, look at what they look at. Feel their wonder at the flowers, an earthworm, the big puddle in the sidewalk or the snowbank at the side of the driveway.

What are your favorite learning activities? How can you incorporate them into your life?

The bow that's always bent will quickly break;
But if unstrung will serve you at your need.
So let the mind some relaxation take
To come back to its task
with fresher heed.
— *Phaedrus*

Refresh

This section includes suggestions for releasing and preventing daily stress
buildup.

Aromatherapy

The effects of scents are often over-
looked in coping with stress. Two of my
favorite scents are roses and citrus.
Roses remind me of romance, gardens
and beauty. A pillow scented with roses
can be very relaxing. Citrus is a refreshing, revitalizing scent. It makes me want
to get up and accomplish things. Lavender and spiced apple scents are said to
be soothing and can lower blood pressure for some people.

What are some of your favorite scents?
How do they make you feel?

But, soft!
methinks I scent
the morning air.
– William Shakespeare

Bathing Rituals

I'm a great believer in baths. On a cool evening, I'll draw a wonderful warm bubble bath, place some relaxing music nearby and soak away the day. If I've allowed frustrations to overwhelm me somewhat, I'll visualize the unpleasantness of the day swirling down the drain with the water at the end of the bath. This will usually allow me to rid myself of "leftover troubles."

Note: Keep the environment in mind when bathing or showering. Use shower heads that reduce the amount of water used.

Bubble Baths

My three favorite bubble baths are chamomile for a restful bath, peppermint to pick me up and eucalyptus when I have a cold. The scent, feel and sounds of a bubble bath are wonderful. I'm always amazed when I meet someone, usually a male, who has never experienced the joys of a bubble bath. Watching rainbows slide down the large bubbles, listening to the delicate popping of the bubbles as they release tiny explosions of scent and pressing a handful of the bubbles between your hands all add extra enjoyment to the bath.

Bubble baths can also be shared with a loved one. It doubles the pleasure when you share the sensations.

Have you ever tried a bubble bath by candlelight? It's exquisite. Add some soft music and you have the makings of a romantic bathing experience either for yourself or to be shared with a loved one. Vary the amount of light by the number of candles.

How far this little candle throws his beams.
– William Shakespeare

Note: Ensure the candles are not in a position to start a fire or your relaxing time will be anything but!

Citrus

One of my friends has sensitive skin and is unable to take bubble baths. If you have a similar problem, try adding some lemon slices to the bath water. You get a wonderful aroma and the lemon makes the water revitalizing.

Hot Tub /Jacuzzi / Whirlpool

These are popular, especially for aching muscles. Be careful that you don't stay in too long (ten minutes maximum) and that the tub you are using is cleaned and tested regularly. Also, be sure to shower afterward.

Caution: Be aware that these are not recommended for people who have diabetes, heart trouble, high blood pressure or nerve impairment or if you are pregnant.

Quiet

In general, I shower to clean and bathe to relax. When I bathe, therefore, I prefer either quiet or soft music and no interruptions. I do not answer the phone. While I was looking after Jonathan's cat, Atticus, I found that my bath time became a source of stress rather relaxation. The cat did not understand how I could prefer to be in the bath rather than playing with him! Because of his incessant meowing at the door, I left the bath in utter frustration instead of in a mellow mood. After a few days of this, I finally learned to pop him into the spare bedroom while I took my bath. He would curl up and sleep in his nest under the bed and I would enjoy my bath. We remain friends.

Toys

You are never too old to have bath toys. A rubber duck can take you out of the realm of everyday into the pleasures of good clean fun. (Excuse the pun.) Sheena has a cute wind-up tug boat that I invariably play with whenever I stay with her. Another friend has a bright

yellow duckie. A touch of whimsy in
the bathroom leads to smiles.

Shower

A friend from work does not like baths;
give her a shower every time. Showers
are great for getting that really clean
feeling. It will help to wake you up in
the morning or ease the transition from
work to home in the evening. And, of
course, it's a great place to sing! They
make shower-proof songbooks now.
Who knows, you may increase your repertoire.

Try some of the scented shower gels.
They are somehow more sensuous than
soap.

**What are some of your favorite
bathing rituals?**

Books/Magazines

Without books and magazines, life would be much more boring, and we would be less interesting people. I consider books to be my friends. The words of the author and my imagination combine to transport me to a multitude of countries, worlds and situations.

Books help to focus your mind and keep it flexible and thinking.

Books are the quietest and most constant of friends; they are the most accessible and wisest of counsellors, and the most patient of teachers.
– Charles W. Eliot

Art

It is wonderful to sit leafing through a book on art; to see the great paintings and sculptures and buildings of the world, to take in the beauty, color, forms.

To add a library to a house is to give that house a soul.
– Cicero

Children's

Children's books are marvellous. A couple of shelves of books which I received as a child prove that I didn't seem to have quite the same reverence for books then as I do now: a number of them have colorful crayon "art" scribbled across the words. However, I do remember loving to read as a child. What were your childhood favorites?

It is well to read everything of something, and something of everything.
– Henry Broughan

Classics

Once I spent a summer reading classics. Some of these were truly enjoyable, while others I found difficult to keep reading to the end. Charles Dickens is fascinating with his twists and coincidences. Homer is challenging but that's all part of the fun.

Fun, Goofy

Fun books and magazines can really brighten your day. A children's book of jokes can be hilarious. Do you remember being delighted with such groaners as "What weighs almost nothing, yet you can't hold it? – Your breath." or "Why did the nurse tiptoe to the medicine cabinet? – She didn't want to wake the sleeping pills." Next time you're at the library, browse through the children's section as well as the humor section. Don't be surprised if a few chuckles escape you.

Interesting Topics

Find magazines or books on topics that interest you and read to your heart's content. Think about a topic that fascinates you but that you've never really managed to get around to researching.

Books come to my call and return when I desire them; they are never out of humor and they answer all my questions with readiness. Some present in review before me the events of past ages; others reveal to me the secrets of Nature. These teach me how to live, and those how to die; these dispel my melancholy with their mirth, and amuse me by their sallies of wit. Some there are who prepare my soul to suffer everything, to desire nothing, and to become thoroughly acquainted with itself. In a word, they open the door to all the arts and sciences.
– Petrarch

Pop in to the library and see what you can find out.

Magazines

When I mention magazines as stress relievers, I don't necessarily mean journals or magazines connected to your work, unless this helps you to unwind. I remember an episode of Star Trek where Scotty was sitting reading "journals" related to engineering. Kirk told Scotty that he was on leave and should be enjoying himself. Scotty looked up completely baffled by Kirk's attitude and said, "But that's what I am doing." Do what relaxes you.

I thoroughly enjoy magazines on interior design, wildlife, painting, inspiration and beauty. One of my favorite magazines is *Victoria*. It has beautiful photography and uplifting articles. There is never an article on the latest disease, abuse, war or famine. It's not that I avoid this knowledge. It's just not something I want to read about when I'm relaxing.

Picture

Picture books aren't just for children. *Canada, A Year of the Land* is a glorious picture book on the four seasons of Canada. There are amazing photographs from across Canada. It's almost like looking at someone's photo album. My latest acquisition in picture books is called *Incredible Light* by Jeffrey Hines. It captures unique natural lighting effects in glorious color.

What is your favorite reading for relaxation?

Breathing

Breathing is a natural act, one we are pretty good at. We all do it constantly. When you pay attention to your breathing you can get an idea of whether or not it is deep or shallow.

To ensure good health:
Eat lightly,
breathe deeply,
live moderately,
cultivate cheerfulness,
and maintain an
interest in life.
– William Louder

When I first became aware of mine, I was surprised to realize how shallow it was. I made a conscious effort to breathe from my diaphragm. It was amazing. By the simple act of slowing and deepening my breaths, I felt calmer and more in control.

In slow, deep breathing from the diaphragm, your tummy should move up and down each time you inhale and exhale, respectively. When you are in a situation that makes you nervous, consciously take four deep breaths. It will help to relieve the anxiety.

Occasionally when I'm having trouble getting to sleep, I'll start a four breath count routine. I start to count each exhale – one, two, three, four. Then I start again at one. Just by counting and becoming aware, my breaths deepen and slow down. This frequently soothes me into sleep.

Another good breathing technique is to consciously make your exhalation slower than your inhalation. In *Take a Deep Breath*, doctors Loehr and Migdow recommend a four count inhale and an eight count exhale. It really does help to calm you.

Concentration

Concentration is my motto – first honesty, then industry, then concentration.
– Andrew Carnegie

Get your mind off your troubles and onto something else for a while. Sometimes we get into a rut and focus too much on our own problems. It happens to everyone on occasion. One way to snap yourself out of the gloom is to get your mind concentrating on something else. Often this can break the cycle of worry. When you stop worrying about the problem, it's often easier to find solutions to it.

Another way to overcome your troubles is to decide to focus your attention on *one* problem, finding as many workable solutions as possible to it. Jot down all your ideas. Then look at your list and decide which action(s) feels right for you and the problem.

As the gardener, by severe pruning, forces the sap of the tree into one or two vigorous limbs, so should you stop off your miscellaneous activity and concentrate your force on one or a few problems.
– Ralph Waldo Emerson

Brainteasers

This is a quick technique I use at work. When I become stuck or sluggish with a project, I'll take a quick five minute break and pull out a book of brainteasers. By focusing my mind on something totally different for this short period of time, I can usually return to the task at hand with a fresher outlook.

Involvement

Volunteer to help out a favorite cause or charity. Help out a friend who is in need, whether it is raking the leaves or stopping by for a chat. Being involved with helping others is healthy.

Massage

Massages are wonderful. You can learn how to give them to yourself and others. You can have a friend give one to you. You can go to a professional masseuse. Make sure you go to a reputable establishment. Getting a massage should ease stress not cause more!

Foot

On those days when I've been on my feet a lot, I'll sit down at the end of the day and place a foot on my lap where I will spend some happy moments massaging it. Then I give the other one equal time. When I'm really lucky, Jonathan will massage my feet for me. It is, of course, reciprocal.

Ideally massage would be part of each day. Wouldn't it be lovely?
– Anne Kent Rush

Full Body

Imagine lying on your tummy having someone gently massage your muscles, giving extra attention to those that feel tight. This is a situation where you need someone's assistance. If you are uncomfortable going to a professional establishment, take a class with a friend. You will be glad you did as you exchange massages with each other.

Neck and Shoulders

One of my colleagues at work frequently gets tight neck and shoulder muscles from working at the computer on tight deadlines. Whenever I consult

him on his area of expertise, I thank him
by giving him a quick shoulder rub.
Lately he's been coming by to ask if I
have any questions he can answer!

Scalp

To me, one of the best parts about having my hair cut is the washing. I thoroughly enjoy lying back and letting
someone wash my hair. Lately I've no-
ticed that not only is my hair washed
with beautifully scented shampoo, there
is also some extra time spent massaging
my scalp. Bliss! It's quite easy to give
yourself a scalp massage. Gently rotate
your fingertips along your scalp apply-
ing as much pressure as is comforting to
you.

Five-Minute Breathers

Taking five minutes for a quick breather
can often send you back to the task at
hand refreshed and more alert. Some
days, it's nice to take five minutes just to
sit and breathe deeply.

*People are always good
company when they are
doing what they really
enjoy.
– Samuel Butler*

Unusual Uses List

Choose an everyday item and then list
all the unusual uses you can think of for
it. For example, what could you do with
rubber bands? Exercise your fingers. Tie
the bands together for a rope or large

slingshot. Cut them into little pieces to stuff a pillow. Wrap them around and around and around each other to create a ball. Paint them bright colors and glue them onto a canvas for a unique three dimensional picture. Make jewellry with them.

Go for it. Choose an everyday item and think of some unusual uses.

Groceries List

Keep a running list each week. Let anyone in the household add to it as they notice needed items. This helps to keep you on track when you go to the store. The list should be in a place accessible to all. My friend, Ann, dislikes grocery shopping, especially weekend mega-shopping. So, she goes to the grocery store every other day or so with her short "running list." She finds that her cupboards are usually well stocked and she spends a minimum of time in the store.

Favorite Foods List

Do you entertain a lot or even a little? Do any of your friends have food allergies or likes and dislikes? Try keeping a notebook with names and favorite foods. Believe me, it helps when you plan that dinner party.

Favorite Restaurants List

Do you enjoy going out to eat? Try keeping a list of your favorite restaurants. Put down the date you were there, the types of foods served, and the price range. Next time you are trying to remember where you had that great Greek meal, you can look it up on your list. You may want to keep a separate list of restaurants that you don't like and why.

Five-Minute Breathers List

Make a list of your own five-minute breathers. What are some of the things you could do to give yourself a mini-break from the routine? Some items from my list include giving a hug (which almost automatically means I also get to receive a hug, unless I'm hugging a stuffed animal or stuffed shirt), reading a few quotations, singing a song, looking at a picture, listening to a music box, doodling, writing a quick "thinking of you" postcard, watching the sunrise.

Menus

Plan an extravagant party. Invite anyone you wish, from the Mad Hatter to your favorite singer to your next door neighbor. Imagine that you can afford anything from flying your guests to a tropical island which you bought for the party to having a world famous chef at your beck and call. What would you serve? If you had a theme, what would it be? How would your food and your theme tie together? What sorts of decorations would you have?

Plan a menu for your dream or theme restaurant. There is a restaurant in Kalispell, Montana called the Bulldog Pub which has one of the most amusing menus I've ever seen. It includes such items as "Saddle of Mule (with or without stirrups), $999.50" and "BBQ'd Worry Wart, $50.00/trauma."

Plan some real "emergency" menus for when you are sick with the flu or a group stays longer than expected. Have some quick and easy ideas and fixings at your fingertips.

Getaways

Getaways can be in your mind as well as for "real." There are times when getting away helps to restore your sanity as well as your soul. Your get away may be on your own or with a friend or loved one. Getaways can be quick or take a week or more; do whatever is necessary for you. Some suggested getaways are an aquarium, an art gallery, a flea market, a farmer's market, a botanical garden, a country drive, a picnic, a retreat.

What are some of your favorite getaways?

It is important from time to time to slow down, to go away by yourself, and simply Be.
– Eileen Caddy

Good Deed

Doing good is a wonderful feeling. It doesn't have to be showy – in fact, it's better if it isn't. It doesn't have to be a grand gesture, a small one is appreciated just as much. Call that friend, smile at someone who looks as though they could use a smile, give a compliment. Basically, just being nice can sometimes be considered to be a good deed. Remember the old rule of doing one good deed every day? Try to follow it and multiply it whenever possible.

Help thy brother's boat across, and lo thine own has reached the shore.
– Hindu Proverb

The smallest good deed is better than the grandest good intention.
– Duguet

Do Unto Others

Being kind and thoughtful gives a peaceful glow which counteracts stress.

The Golden Rule is of no use to you whatever unless you realize that it is your move.
– Dr. Frank Crane

It is one of the beautiful compensations of life that no man can sincerely try to help another, without helping himself.
– Gamaliel Bailey

Happiness is a by-product of an effort to make some- one else happy.
– Grettal Brooker Palmer

When you rise in the morning, form a resolution to make the day a happy one to a fellow-creature.
– Sydney Smith

If you have not felt the joy of doing a kind act, you have neglected much, and most of all yourself.
– A. Neilen

Invite a friend to tea. Send a postcard of your city to an out-of-town friend who would enjoy seeing where you live. Send a postcard to someone in the same city just for fun. Send a "thinking of you" note, card or postcard.

Do you know someone who is shut-in or ill? Go for a visit. See if they would like to go for a drive or an easy walk. Maybe just going for a drive around the neighborhood would make their day.

Tell a friend all the nice things about them that you like. Compliment a col- league at work or a family member. Re- member that sincerity counts.

Volunteer to help out at a local hospital, food bank, soup kitchen, geriatrics home or your favorite charity.

Write a thank-you note or letter to a friend or to a waitress or store clerk who was especially helpful.

What are some gestures that the people in your life would appreciate?

Hugs

I think if I'm addicted to anything, it's to hugs. I adore giving and receiving hugs. You can tell a lot about a person by the way in which they hug. Sometimes you can tell that they really are glad to see you, missed you lately, have a lot on their minds or are upset with you about something just by the way they return your hug. Hugs can be quick or slow. They can be preceded or followed by a kiss. They can be a pat on the back or an "I'm here for you" gesture.

Hugs don't always have to be shared with others. You can also hug a pillow or a teddy bear. These hugs are especially nice when you are feeling blue but aren't ready to talk it out with anyone.

You can hug a tree, a glowing report, an uplifting book or a shirt scented with your loved one. While you are spending time with your pet, give a hug. Don't forget to hug yourself as well.

An embrace should fill the heart as well as the arms.
— Hugh Prather

Humor

Laughter is a fantastic stress reliever. When was the last time you had a really good belly laugh where your eyes watered and your cheeks hurt? I find those

Good humor is goodness and wisdom combined.
– Chinese fortune

A good laugh is sunshine in the house.
– Thackeray

People who laugh actually live longer than those who don't laugh. Few persons realize that health actually varies according to the amount of laughter.
– Dr. James J. Walsh

most therapeutic. I don't get them nearly as much as I did when I was younger. Maybe I've started taking life too seriously. I'm more of a giggler with an occasional good "out loud" laugh. I have been known to chortle over a *Herman* treasury or a *Fox Trot* collection. I'm also a pun lover.

Whenever it's appropriate to laugh, go for it. If you are in a situation where you think, "I'll look back on this and laugh someday." Why not make someday now? Jonathan and I had one of "those" trips once. The kind where a LOT of little things went wrong: the plane was late, some young children were seated nearby who were having a screaming match, the luggage took forever to arrive, the shuttle bus which we called for left without us, the airport parking service where we left the car didn't have a booster service (the temperature was -32°C when we arrived home), there was a twelve-hour wait for tow trucks, the taxi we finally got had to stop for gas but couldn't get the pump nozzle to fit into the tank. By this time I was giggling in the back seat of the cab as it was just too funny. We did get home and the next day retrieved our car from the airport without incident. Giggling was a lot more fun than getting angry or depressed.

Try looking at the world as if you were assigned the task of writing a sketch for a stand-up comic. It's amazing how differently you see things.

The most thoroughly wasted of all days is that on which one has not laughed.
– Chanfort

What are some ways you could get more laughter into your life?

Meditation/Relaxation

Meditation can be a quick breathing exercise or a full blown deep relaxation session. It can include audio tapes or biofeedback machines. You can meditate while staring into a candle flame, watching the clouds in the sky or the waves on a beach. Once you master the art of meditation you can call upon it at any time to give you a sense of inner peace and control of self.

When we learn to relax the body, breath, and mind, the body becomes healthy, the mind becomes clear, and our awareness becomes balanced.
– Tarthang Tulku

Whenever possible, ensure that you will not be interrupted while meditating or doing a relaxation exercise. Get into a comfortable position, either sitting or lying down. Unplug the phone or have the machine answer it.

Autogenic Training

This is the relaxation technique I started with. You focus your attention on one body part at a time. For example, focus on your right arm. Then silently amd slowly repeat to yourself, "My arm is heavy." "My arm is heavy and limp. My arm is letting go." Do this with each part of your body until your feel the relaxation in each muscle. After daily practice, you can get to the point where just thinking about the phrases can relax your muscles. This form of relaxation was developed by doctors Johannes Schultz and Wolfgang Luthe. You can change the phrases to suit yourself. For example, you might prefer the phrase "My arm is warm and limp."

A man of meditation is happy, not for an hour or a day, but quite round the circle of his years.
– Isaac Taylor

Progressive Relaxation

Progressive relaxation is yet another technique for relaxing. In this method, you tense each part of your body in turn and then relax it. It is designed to show you maximum contrast between your relaxed state and your tense state. It is frequently combined with soothing music.

Relaxation Response

The Relaxation Response is a method developed by Dr. Herbert Benson. This technique requires you to sit comfortably and breathe naturally. Each time you exhale, think of the word "one." Try to keep this as the only thought in your mind. If other thoughts intrude, acknowledge them and then let go of them. Remain passive. Do this for about ten to twenty minutes.

Other methods include saying a specific sound or word on exhalations during deep breathing. For example, breathe deeply for two breaths. On the third deep breath, softly say "ooooo" during a slow exhalation. Repeat this three-breath procedure three times. You may want to try different sounds to find one which feels good for you.

Another style of meditation is to stare at an object for a period of time. While doing this, focus your entire attention on the object.

Meditation is the life of the soul; action is the soul of meditation.
– Francis Quarles

Try lying down comfortably for about five minutes. During those five minutes, your task is to ensure that you do not move. Just scan your body, becoming aware of how it feels in this state. I find that I invariably develop an itchy spot when doing this. I've managed to prog-

A quiet mind cureth all.
– Robert Burton

ress to a stage where I can usually "will" the itch away and remain motionless for the five minutes. This kind of activity (or should I say, non-activity) is good for finding tense spots in your body. You don't have to lie down for it. You can be still while sitting at the office or standing in line. Mentally scan your body to see how it's feeling. Where are your tense spots? Do this a few times a day for a week or so. It will help you to discover where your "hot" spots are. Once you know them, you can give them special attention with exercises, massage, stretches and preventive measures.

Note: Whenever you do a relaxation or meditation exercise, be sure to come out of it slowly. Allow yourself some time to become aware of the world again.

What meditation or relaxation styles work best for you?

Within you there is a stillness and sanctuary to which you can retreat at anytime and be by yourself.
– Hermann Hesse

Music

Music is wonderful – it can mirror our feelings or bring us out of a blue mood. Try some of the pieces listed in the Sources section. Some are soothing while others are energizing.

We are the music makers,
We are the dreamers
of dreams.
– Arthur O'Shaughnessy

Conduct

Play the *1812 Overture* by Tchaikovsky and pretend that you are the conductor. It makes for a great upper body workout as well as being just plain fun.

But I struck one chord of
music,
Like the sound of a great
Amen.
– Adelaide Ann Procter

Dance

Dance around the place to your favorite pieces. When the music is playing, ask for the pleasure of this dance from your sweetheart, child, parent, or friend. Dance graciously or boogie to the beat. (For more dance ideas, see the "Activate" chapter.)

On with the dance!
let joy be unconfined . . .
– Lord Byron

Psychologists have found
that music does things to
you whether you like it or
not. Fast tempos invariably
raise your pulse, respira-
tion, and blood pressure;
slow music lowers them.
– Doron K. Antrim

Listen

I have a collection of music boxes, most of which have a story or memory behind them. When I play some of them, I release a big sigh and a soft smile steals across my face. With others, I start laughing or singing along. They have become friends.

Take a music bath once or
twice a week for a few sea-
sons, and you will find that
it is to the soul what the
water-bath is to the body.
– Oliver Wendell Holmes

My music collection is rather eclectic but with strong tendencies towards classical selections. Having a wide variety of music allows me to suit the music to my mood or to change my mood by my choice of music.

Play

Jonathan has joined an adult band class where he gets an opportunity to play his flute. He gets away from the regular routine, meets people and has fun playing the instrument of his choice. Miju, the cockatiel, sometimes joins in when Jonathan is practicing.

Sing

It's the song you sing and wear that makes the sun shine everywhere.
– J. W. Riley

Everyone suddenly burst out singing.
– Seigfried Sassoon

Singing is one of the most rewarding ways for me to release stress. Whether it's belting out a song in the shower or humming a sad song, singing seems to be able to reflect my mood and bring me out of sadness or depression. One of my favorite songbooks is *The World's Best Funny Songs* by Esther L. Nelson. It contains childhood favorites such as "John Jacob Jingleheimer Schmidt," "On Top of My Pizza" and "The Cat Came Back."

Pets

Pets can be soothing *and* irritating. The same cat that curls up purring on my lap on a cool autumn evening can drive me to distraction on a summer's day when he continuously yowls to be on the other side of the door. However, the soothing far outweighs the annoyance. Spending time with your pets is rewarding. Watching fish swimming in an aquarium is considered to be very calming.

Pussy said to the Owl, "You elegant fowl! How charmingly sweet you sing!"
— Edward Lear

Priorities

If you find that you have no time for the things you want to do, take a look at the demands on your time. Make a list of the things you do on a daily/weekly/monthly basis. Once you have your list completed, take a long hard look at it. What on the list could be put to the back burner of your time? How important is it for you and your sense of well-being that you do everything on the list?

What are some shortcuts you could take? For example, if you wash and wax your floors weekly, could you buy a product that does both those steps in one process? What about washing weekly and waxing every other week? Rather than ironing every day, could

The art of being wise is the art of knowing what to overlook.
– William James

you rearrange your closets so that you could iron once a week without losing the crispness? For myself, I would much rather spend some time reading than cleaning. So, my apartment cleaning gets done once a week. I often give quick swipes to problem areas like the chrome in the bathroom. This makes the bathroom look better and makes it easier to keep the faucets shiny during the major clean.

What are some areas of your "to do" list that could be cut back?

Quiet Time

The miracle comes quietly into the mind that stops an instant and is still.
– A Course in Miracles

Aim for some quiet time every day. This doesn't have to be a marathon session, even five minutes a day will help. Use the time to regroup, regenerate, think about pleasant things or don't think at all. Let everyone know when your quiet time is and that it is not to be disturbed. Ensure that you do not disturb others' quiet times.

What can you do to arrange for some quiet time in your days?

It is an experiment worth trying to be alone and to be quiet for a brief period every day. Under city conditions it may be difficult to carry out, but most of us could do it if we tried. At any rate, we should moderate the pace at which we are living. If we remain in high gear, at top pressure, we are bound to suffer fatigue and strain.
— Robert J. McCracken

See/Watch

Take some time to really see the world around you. Pull off to the side of the road, stop and watch the colors of the rainbow or that lightning show being put on free of charge (excuse the pun). Look at the children playing and listen to their squeals of joy and delight at being alive. Watch the horses in the field as they frolic about in the warmth of a spring day. Go birdwatching.

Still — in a way — nobody sees a flower — really — it is so small — we haven't time — and to see takes time, like to have a friend takes time.
— Georgia O'Keeffe

Jonathan and I have driven out of our way on occasion to pull off by the side of a dark country road so that we can stare up at the stars in the night sky. We were delighted one evening when the Northern lights joined the stars and danced across the sky in an ephemeral display.

Slow Down

Hurry is only good for catching flies.
— Russian Proverb

There is more to life than increasing its speed.
— Mahatma Ghandi

Slow down and enjoy life. It's not only the scenery you miss by going too fast — you also miss the sense of where you are going and why.
— Eddie Cantor

Remember that saying, "The hurrier I go the behinder I get." Take time to breathe. Take five minutes for walking away from the job or smelling a flower or just for sitting down. Five minutes may not seem like much but it does help.

Give guilt a holiday. For some of us, it's a much needed holiday! You deserve a break. It's not morally wrong to take time out to refresh yourself. Of course, if you are taking five minutes out of every seven, then maybe you're going a bit overboard. Moderation is the key word. As someone once said, moderation in everything, including moderation!

Smiles

A smile is the whisper of a laugh.
— Unknown

Wear a smile and have friends; wear a frown and have wrinkles. What do we live for if not to make the world less difficult for each other?
— George Eliot

Smile wider and more often. It makes an amazing difference to your attitude. See how many strangers you can make smile by smiling at them. Look as though you have a happy secret. It gives those around you something interesting to think about.

Stress-Free Hat

Assign a special, favorite, goofy, gorgeous and/or hideous hat as your stress-free hat. When it's on your head it shelters you from all stresses. You are not allowed to worry about a thing. No one can come to you with a problem while you are wearing this hat (unless it's an emergency like the cockatiel has the cat's tail in his beak and has no intention of letting go).

Stress Rock

Find an interesting rock or sea shell. One that appeals to you. Mine is rounded and smooth. Carry it with you, or give it a special place at work or home. You may have more than one stress rock.

Maybe if I listen closely
to the rocks
Next time, I'll hear
something, if not
A word, perhaps the
faint beginning of
a syllable.
— Phoebe Hanson

When you have worries, tell them to your rock and let it carry the load. Sometimes I will carry a stress rock in my pocket when I'm doing something that isn't comfortable for me. When I begin to get stressed out, I just reach in and manipulate the stress rock in my hand and it somehow soothes me. (My stress rock is named Seenmore because it has probably "seen more" than any living thing.)

Stretch

First thing before I get out of bed in the morning I stretch my body. It feels glorious. When I've been working intensely at the computer for a long period of time, I will suddenly realize how sore my shoulders and neck are. A few good stretches and I'm soon back in order. I also have a set of neck and shoulder exercises from my doctor. They are marvellous. When I do them regularly, my neck and shoulders feel wonderful. A great shoulder exercise is the shrug. Do this ten or twenty times, breathing in as you pull your shoulders up to your ears and exhaling as you drop them back down. Your shoulders will thank you.

Take Time

Take time for yourself and for being with those you love and care about. If taking time for yourself is difficult because of commitments to family, then try to work out a buddy system. Have a friend or neighbor look after your children, aged parent, or pets for an hour or two or a weekend. Be prepared to do the same for them.

If you find it difficult because of conflicting schedules to get together with your friends and family, make dates or have tea parties where you can invite a few friends at once. A friend of mine is taking classes, teaching classes and running an independent consulting firm. She finds the best way to ensure that she has time for her teenagers is to make a date to take them out to dinner. It makes it a treat as well as giving them time to talk.

You are the only one who can give yourself the gift of time.
– Alexandra Stoddard

Tea Ceremony

I am notorious for pouring water straight from the kettle into my mug and dunking the tea bag a few times. That's my cup of tea ready. (My British relatives would probably disown me!)

There are few hours in life more agreeable than the hour dedicated to the ceremony known as afternoon tea.
– Henry James

However, when I do take the time to brew the tea "properly" using the teapot with its knitted cosy and then graciously pouring myself a cup of tea into a favorite cup and saucer, I feel special. It's as though I have acknowledged that I, too, deserve that extra attention that I generally give only to guests.

Your choice of drinking utensil says something about what you feel you deserve. At work, I have a water mug I use almost constantly. Written on it are such phrases as *Believe in yourself. Create peace. Seek truth. Embark on adventure.* My tea mug, given to me by my sister many years ago, has a goofy set of owls spanning its perimeter. It's special for sentimental reasons.

The department I work employs over 50 people. One of our activities throughout the year is the "Cookie Club." Anyone is welcome but there is no pressure to join (well, very little). As a member you are treated to cookies, cakes, cupcakes, squares, tarts and so on every Wednesday for afternoon coffee break. The only dues are that about three times a year, it's someone's turn to bring the goodies.

It's a great club. The conversations that arise during these afternoon feasts range from work-related difficulties, recipe swaps, pet information, home decorating tips, holidays, interesting articles, politics, or whatever is current in the news of the world, the country, the province or on campus. These talks usually stay fairly light but there have been some serious discussions as well. It has become a ritual which helps to keep the great variety of people who work in the department in touch. Besides which, it's fun.

Toys

A stuffed toy is comforting. Playing with building toys can be engrossing. Just letting go and having fun relieves stress.

Take some time to wander through a toy store. If something in your price range really catches your eye, why don't you indulge in it? If it makes you feel better, you can always pretend you are buying it for a child.

Over the past few years I've managed to allow myself to buy a BIG box of crayons (64 colors), a kaleidoscope, pick-up sticks, bubble makers, and some small water pistols. Each purchase was inexpensive but has given hours of fun. Jonathan and I have had great fun sneaking up on each other with loaded water pistols.

I turned to Archibald, my safe old bear, Whose woolen eyes looked sad or glad at me, Whose ample forehead I could wet with tears, Whose half moon ears received my confidence, Who made me laugh, who never let me down. I used to wait for hours to see him move, Convinced that he could breathe.
– The Green Tiger Press Greeting Card

Treat Yourself

$5 Treat

Every once in awhile, take five dollars (or whatever amount you can spare) and go out and buy something fun with it. It could be bubble blowing mix, a couple of magazines or comic books, a big box of crayons, a fun pen or pencil, or a pretty poster. Whatever you decide to spend the five dollars on, it should be something you want which you wouldn't ordinarily buy for yourself. Remember this is a treat.

Pamper Yourself

Always leave enough room in your life to do something that makes you happy, satisfied, or even joyous.
– Paul Hawken

Pamper yourself at least once a day. This can be anything that pleases you. My treats include bubble baths, browsing in book stores, smiling, hugs, gazing at favorite pictures, having J. Higby's Chocolate Thunder frozen yogurt, reading, having a bowl of popcorn, talking with Jonathan, having a good giggle, petting the cat, whistling to the bird, watching Winnie the Pooh cartoons, reading the Saturday comics, eating raisin oatmeal cookies . . .

What can you do to pamper yourself every day?

Vacation

Vacations are wonderful. They can be long or short in duration. A friend of mine treats one weekend every month as a mini-vacation. Throughout the week on her mini-vacation weekends, she does as much of the cleaning and shopping as possible to leave the weekend free. On the mini-vacation weekends, she makes dates with friends for tea, lunch or whatever. She'll visit art galleries or museums. She'll spend Saturday morning at the library and then the rest of the weekend on a reading binge.

You may not be able to take a full weekend but maybe you could take Saturday morning as your mini-vacation. Put the answering machine on, tell your family that you are on vacation for the morning and do your own thing. Maybe sleeping in and then eating a leisurely brunch while watching your favorite love story is your cup of tea. Or maybe you want to be able to get away from the house for the morning, walk in a park by yourself, stop for a cup of tea and play a rousing game of squash. Or maybe it's taking time to play with your favorite hobby uninterrupted. Remember to enjoy yourself. Remember, too, that others in your family deserve to have this privilege.

Real full-blown vacations are also important. Get away from it all if you possibly can. If "all" includes the family, which it sometimes can, then plan separate vacations with the kids going to camp or visiting relatives or friends and you meeting up with them later. Even if it's just a couple of days, it can refresh you. On the other hand, maybe you find you don't have enough time with your family and want more. In that case, plan a family holiday where you can be together.

Visualize

Visualizing is a technique which can be mastered by anyone. For some, it comes quickly and easily. For others, it takes practice. It is well worth the effort.

Let the walls of your mind be filled with many beautiful pictures.
– William Lyon Phelps

Visualizing is relaxing and seeing pictures in your mind's eye. It is excellent for relieving stress because it allows you to remove yourself mentally from the stressful situation. It can also be used for mentally seeing a stressful situation being resolved. You can work through different approaches to a problem in your mind using visualization techniques.

There are many books and tapes on visualizing. Some of these are listed in the Sources section. Some of my favorite techniques follow.

The rainbows of the mind brighten the skies of our life with color, grace and contrast against stormy clouds.
– Joyce Wycoff

When I am to do something that causes me stress, such as teaching a class for the first time or having an interview or meeting someone for the first time, I will often visualize the situation in my mind, like a mini-movie. I always ensure that the movie has a positive outcome. The best times that I have found for doing this are just as I am falling asleep, just as I am waking and just prior to the event.

Another technique is finding a positive and relaxing place in my mind. This is a totally private place because I don't have to let anyone into it. Even if I describe it to someone else, they still cannot intrude upon me when I am there unless I visualize letting them enter.

For years now I've been building a house near the ocean with a wraparound porch, sun deck, craft room, rose garden, kitchen garden and wildflower garden. There are stained glass windows and etched and bevelled windows and French doors and arches throughout. The floor plan has changed dramatically a few times but that's okay. The house is in my head. Building, remodelling and decorating it has been a source of pleasure for years. Some nights it eases me to sleep.

Another place which I visualize for relaxation is a tropical beach area. There's a large, comfortable hammock slung between two palms. Nearby is lush tropical growth with a small waterfall which forms into a pleasant babbling stream winding down to the ocean. The ocean is within quick walking distance and its

Five minutes, just before going to sleep, given to a bit of directed imagination regarding achievement possibilities of the morrow, will steadily and increasingly bear fruit, particularly if all ideas of difficulty, worry, or fear are resolutely ruled out and replaced by those of accomplishment and smiling courage.
– Frederick Pierce

rhythmic waves soothe me. Since this is a tropical fantasy, I have added an aura around my body which no insects can penetrate. This ensures that I can relax while there.

I can also visualize letting certain people into a lovely sitting room in my mind. This room is where I mentally invite people when we have problems to work through. I imagine what I would say to them and how they might react. I never leave this mental room while still feeling angry or upset with the person(s) involved. It's amazing how often I can resolve *my* difficulties with a person or situation in this manner.

What are the refreshing things you do for yourself? What can you do for others?

Care For

The preservation of health is a duty.
Few seem conscious that there is
such a thing as physical
morality.
— Herbert Spencer

Care For

Caring for yourself, as defined here, includes both emotional and physical health. Personal well-being includes everything from getting enough sleep to eating properly. It's how you view yourself, how you talk to yourself and what you expect of yourself.

Every man is a builder of a temple called his body.
– Henry David Thoreau

When you don't feel well, even small things can become stressful. Making the effort to look after yourself will pay great dividends in the long run. Find a lifestyle that suits you and keeps you healthy. For some people, this is exercising daily, eating only fruits, vegetables and grains and avoiding alcoholic beverages. For others it means cutting back on fatty foods, exercising a few times a week, eating more fruit. Do what feels right for you. You will know it when you find it. You feel more energetic, your hair and skin will glow and you will be calmer in stressful situations.

Emotional Well-being

Your emotional well-being includes how you handle stressful situations. How you handle your anger, your frustrations, your joy. Loving yourself leads to a more peaceful, calmer outlook on life in general.

Safeguard the health of both body and soul.
– Cleobulus

Affirmations

Affirmations are ways of telling yourself things are okay. Always phrase your affirmations in the positive. For example, instead of telling yourself not to forget something, tell yourself to remember it. If you are having difficulties in a certain area of your life, create a positive affirmation about it that you can repeat to yourself whenever needed. Say things like: "I am healthy and strong," "I am courageous and able to handle this," "I am in control of my life," "I am filling my life with joy and laughter."

When you are in a stressful situation, taking a deep breath and telling yourself that you can handle things can really help.

Belief

One needs something to believe in, something for which one can have whole-hearted enthusiasm.
– Hannah Senesh

Faith is the root of all blessings.
– Jeremy Taylor

I'm of the opinion that everyone benefits from a belief in a Higher Power. I also believe that everyone needs to find their own method of belief and worship. My personal belief has seen me through some pretty rough times. It has always been there for me and I have faith that it will sustain me through the rest of my life as well.

Because belief is so very personal, I will leave the rest of this section blank for you to fill in. I'm frequently amazed at how often we know we believe but have a difficult time expressing just what it is that we believe.

Faith is positive,
enriching life
in the here and now.
— Webb B. Garrison

What do you believe in?

Decision Making

I used to be one of the world's best pro-crastinators when it came to making a decision. I avoided them like the plague. A technique which now helps me is a "Pros, Cons, and Gut Feeling" list.

Decision is a sharp knife
that cuts clean and straight;
indecision is a dull one
that hacks and tears and
leaves ragged edges
behind.
— Gordon Graham

Pros   Cons   Gut Feelings

The percentage of mistakes in quick decisions is no greater than in long-drawn-out vacillations, and the effect of decisiveness itself "makes things go" and creates confidence.
– Anne O'Hare McCormick

Usually I know deep down what I want to do; but, I'm not sure if I should or can do it, so I hesitate. Now I list the pros and cons in my head or on paper and then ask myself, what do I feel about this? What do I want to do? By listing the rational pros and cons as well as adding the gut feelings aspect, I come to decisions more readily.

Another technique is to list all the possible alternatives to a problem. By brainstorming for ideas you often come up with unique and beautiful solutions. Finally making that decision can relieve stress.

Forgive/Forget

Forgiveness saves the expense of anger, the cost of hatred, the waste of spirits.
– Hannah More

Do you have any grudges or resentments lingering in your heart and mind? If so, work at getting rid of them. They are extra stresses which you carry around with you. The sooner you can work them out of your system, the better it will be for you. Sometimes you can work through them by talking with another person to get a fresh perspective. Try putting yourself in the other person's shoes. Sometimes a forgiveness meditation will work. At other times, professional counselling is required.

The heart has always the pardoning power.
– Madame Swetcine

While you are working on this, don't forget to forgive yourself. You are human. Mistakes are part of life. Learn from them, forgive and move on with your life.

Write injuries in dust,
benefits in marble.
– Benjamin Franklin

Friends

Never take your friends for granted. They are precious and help make life interesting and wonderful. Friendships take time to develop and nurture. We need to keep in touch with our friends, not just at holidays but through the entire year. It doesn't take long to write a quick "Hello, I was just thinking about you and smiling" on the back of a postcard. It does brighten that person's day.

Oh, the comfort, the inexpressible comfort, of feeling safe with a person, having neither to weigh thoughts nor measure words, but pouring them all right out, just as they are, chaff and grain together; certain that a faithful hand will take and sift them, keep what is worth keeping, and with a breath of kindness blow the rest away.
– Rex Cole

Share your life with your friends. They can help you see problems from a different perspective. They can rejoice with you when you share your happiness. Don't treat your friends to a negative perspective all the time. It can be very wearing on them.

We read that we ought to forgive our enemies; but we do not read that we ought to forgive our friends.
– Cosimo de Medici

Tell your friends that you like and/or love them. Let them know verbally or in writing.

Sometimes friendships do come to an end, through distance or through differences in growth patterns or something else. If you have tried to keep the friendship going, but it just isn't there anymore, then say goodbye. It is just a natural progression.

The ornaments of a home are the friends who frequent it.
– Emerson

Let Go

There are times when you have to let go of the emotions that are causing you stress by expressing them. Go ahead and cry. Tears can wash away the stress. Mourn the loss of a loved one. Let your sorrow and angers out. My friend, Ken, asked me if I had "howling" in the book. This is something that he found rather useful when he was in university. He said that when things got tough, he'd look up at the sky and howl. If it works – go for it! Look at the situation which is stressing you. Try to see the humor in it. Laugh.

Scream into a pillow to get the anger out. Take a course or read a book on how to express anger. It is important to learn how to let it out in a healthy way. Keeping anger inside isn't healthy. Try writing a letter to the person or thing that is causing you stress. Be as open and harsh as you want to be in the letter. Do NOT send the letter, just pour the pain onto the paper.

Say goodbye to something or someone who hurt you long ago. Don't hang on to old grievances. They will only weigh you down.

Have a pretend conversation with someone or something that is causing you

Tears are blessings,
let them flow.
– Harry Hunter

Laughter and tears are
meant to turn the wheels
of the same sensibility;
one is windpower
and the other
waterpower,
that is all.
– Oliver Wendell Holmes

stress. For example, a colleague at work often frustrates me. I will sometimes hold a conversation in my head between the person and myself. It not only helps me to vent my frustrations, usually it helps me to see another perspective, as well as the humor in the situation.

If you are really annoyed by someone, have a trusted friend role play with you. See how you might be able to work out the situation without being in the intimidating position of really being there. Have your friend tell you where they think you are on track in your approach to the situation and where you might make some improvements. Sometimes, just doing the role play helps you to see the other person's perspective and helps to diffuse your anger and frustration before you actually talk with the person who has annoyed you. You will handle yourself better and feel more in control of the situation if you have practiced removing the emotions from it beforehand.

If your eyes are blinded with your worries, you cannot see the beauty of the sunset.
–Krishnamurti

Perspective

Look at what is bothering you from another point of view. If a person or animal is bothering you, look at the situation from their perspective. If it's a situation which is causing you prob-

Have patience with all things but first of all with yourself.
– St. Francis of Sales

lems, ask a friend how they see it. Sometimes we get too close to a situation to be able to see a way out. I recently asked my friend Jackie to help me with a situation in which I wasn't sure I should get involved. She listened to me and read the letter from the person and gave me some valuable advice. I even followed it! She saw the situation from a fresh perspective and could make suggestions based on that.

Realistic Expectations

Give yourself a chance. Make your expectations of yourself and of others realistic. Check to see what expectations others have of you. Are they realistic? Do they come close to what you want for yourself? If not, how can you change the situation?

Give yourself some goals. Work towards them. Allow yourself to fail and to learn from that. Don't berate yourself for failing. Don't give up when you fail. Learn and go on.

Self-Esteem

The full and joyful acceptance of the worst in oneself is the only sure way of transforming it.
– Henry Miller

Focus on your positive attributes. Acknowledge your weaknesses. Accept yourself, warts and all. You are the best you there is. The best you there will ever be. Work on your weaknesses but don't see only your weaknesses. Accept when you make mistakes. You are human. It comes with the territory. In all likelihood, it means that you are trying and growing. You are stretching your boundaries.

When you focus on the positive and the possibilities you have, things look brighter. Stressful situations are more easily handled when you get into the habit of looking for the positive aspects and the possibilities which might arise from the situation.

Self-Talk

Self-talk is just talking to yourself. We do it all the time. Not necessarily out loud, but in our heads. We have thoughts milling about our heads almost constantly. Stop to listen to those thoughts. Do you praise and encourage yourself or do you fuss at yourself and put yourself down? When you make a mistake, do you call yourself stupid or do you ask what you can learn from the situation? When you do something right, do you praise yourself or do you say it was a fluke?

You may find the worst enemy or the best friend within yourself.
– English Proverb

If you find your self-talk negative most of the time, start changing *now*. Give yourself pats on the back. Praise yourself. Encourage yourself. When you make a mistake, tell yourself that next time you'll do better. When you do something right, tell yourself that you did well.

Support Group/Professional Help

If you are in real distress, find a support group or seek professional help in dealing with your stress. There are numerous groups around which help in specific areas. If you decide on professional help, seek guidance from your family doctor, your church leaders or a professional counselling organization through your work.

No one is wise enough by himself.
– Titus Maccius Plautus

Tolerance/Acceptance

Practice tolerance. The more we can accept ourselves and others around us, the more content we will be. Enjoy the differences among people. Enjoy the sights, sounds, flavors of different cultures. Remember, if you had been brought up in a different culture, you would have different beliefs, too.

The responsibility of tolerance lies with those who have the wider vision.
– George Eliot

What are some things you can do to improve your emotional well-being?

Physical Well-being

Exercise

Exercise is vital to health and an excellent way to control stress. (See Activate chapter.)

Health is the vital principle of bliss, and exercise of health.
– James Thomson

Nutrition

Good nutrition is also vital to good health and reduced stress. By adopting a healthy eating style and sticking to it, your stress coping abilities can develop and strengthen.

Taste is a pleasure that should always be renewed, and a pleasure that should move you on to different levels.
– Michel Guerard

Bake

Baking can be so rewarding. The flavor and aromas are wonderful. Once you have the basics down, you can be inventive. Create your own recipes. I've developed my own cookie recipe. I think they are pretty good and reasonable healthy too. (See Recipe section at the end of this chapter.) When you bake, think about your friends. Would it brighten someone's day if you gave them a portion of the baking? I try to keep some baking in the freezer for those unexpected visitors. I don't always manage to keep the freezer well-stocked as frequently those unexpected visitors end up being me raiding the freezer! Another aspect of baking which I find soothing is decorating cakes and cookies. One Christmas, I was quite ambitious and decided to bake gingerbread people as gifts for my office colleagues. Each cookie was decorated with one or two of the distinguishing characteristics of each person in the office. It was great fun and everyone welcomed themselves! At that time, the office consisted of five people other than myself so it wasn't an outrageous plan. Now I work with over fifty people and wouldn't dream of trying it.

"Nearly eleven o'clock," said Pooh happily. "You're just in time for a little smackerel of something ... "
– A. A. Milne

Cook

To me there is nothing as creative in cooking as making soups, stews, casseroles and salads. It's so much fun to look in the cupboards to see what's available and then put together a new concoction. Of course, sometimes it doesn't exactly turn out right, but once you get the hang of what works well together, you can turn out some masterpieces.

A first-rate soup is more creative than a second-rate painting.
– Abraham Maslow

I frequently make a pot of chicken noodle soup when a friend is ill. I'm not sure if it's the soup itself or the idea that someone cared enough to make it for them that helps. Making soup is not a quick activity. For me, a really good soup needs to simmer away for hours

on the back of the stove. It brings out all
the goodness and flavors. (See Recipe
section at the end of this chapter.)

Eat Well

Find a nutritional plan that suits you.
There are so many "gurus" around with
THE way to eat that this can be stressful
in itself. If you are confused, you are not
alone. If I can give any advice here, it
comes in two words – MODERATION
and VARIETY. Be wary of diets that
focus on one food or food group to the
near exclusion of all others. Check with
a knowledgeable source before embarking upon a complete change in your
diet. Keep your fat intake low and your
fiber intake reasonably high. Eat healthy
foods more than junk foods. If you
don't already eat a lot of fruits and vegetables, try increasing your intake of
these items.

Oh! I Ate them all
And oh!What a
Stomach-ache...
Green stolen apples
– Shiki

Man is what he eats.
– Ludwig Feuerbach

Juices

Fruit juices are some of the most refreshing beverages around. My personal favorites are pineapple/grapefruit,
grapefruit/orange, watermelon and
apple/pear. (See Recipe section at the
end of this chapter.) Vegetable juices are
also very nutritious. If you can make
your own, so much the better. Fresh-
made juices have an extra flavor and

zip. I find that when I make the effort to make my juices with my juicer from scratch rather than from frozen concentrates, my energy level rises.

Try mixing fruit juice with carbonated spring water in equal portions. Add a slice of lemon or a sprig of fresh mint to fancy it up.

Reduce Caffeine

Whenever possible, cut back on the amount of caffeine you ingest. It can make you edgy and nervous. Drinking decaffeinated coffee, tea or cola can help reduce your stress levels. Try to increase your intake of fruit or vegetable juices. Of course, there is the old stand-by, water.

Sleep

*To tired limbs and
over-busy thoughts,
Inviting sleep and soft
forgetfulness.*
– William Wordsworth

*Many fears are born
of fatigue
and loneliness.*
– Max Ehrmann

Get enough sleep. This is really important. GET ENOUGH SLEEP. When you are tired, more things stress you, stress you more and stress you more easily. I'm an eight-hour-per-night person. Some nights I toss and turn and simply cannot get my mind to shut off for the day. Some of the techniques I use then are taking a walk, having a cup of chamomile tea, visualizing each color of the rainbow separately (frequently, I don't make it all the way through before falling asleep), visualizing a dream house or secret place, playing solitaire, adding to my blessings book or reading a book. I thoroughly enjoy Robert Fulghum's books. The chapters are short and usually leave me smiling.

Sleep is the best meditation.
– Dalai Lama

Another technique is to tell myself to come back to the present. Frequently if I'm having difficulty sleeping, it's because I'm thinking about something that might happen in the future or worrying about something I did or didn't do in the past. When I tell myself to live now, I can usually put things into better perspective.

Put off thy cares with thy clothes; so shall thy rest strengthen thy labor, and so shall thy labor sweeten thy rest.
– Francis Quarles

An aspect of "sleeping" which I have changed over the years is how I waken. Instead of a jarring alarm to which my system does not respond well, I awaken to a classical music radio station. It allows me to surface in a calm and what I consider to be a civilized manner.

Take rest, a field that has rested gives a bountiful crop.
– Ovid

The other thing that I stopped doing was listening to the news first thing in the morning or last thing at night. I find that I can face the new day and the night much more calmly this way.

Smoking

If you can't actually stop smoking, then at least make an effort to cut down on the number of cigarettes you smoke. If

Fresh air is more intoxicating than cigarette smoke.
– Beverley Nichols

you have children in the house, make every effort not to smoke near them. This helps to keep their air fresher. You might want to try an air purifier in your home and/or office if necessary.

Some friends have told me that smoking is what reduces their stress – until they start to think about what it is doing to their bodies! If you have a friend or colleague who has managed to stop smoking, ask how they did it. Maybe it will work for you.

Judy's Raisin Drop Cookies

<u>Ingredients</u>
margarine
honey
sugar
egg
baking soda
sea salt (optional)
whole wheat flour
oat bran
wheat germ or oats
cinnamon
nutmeg
raisins

Cream: ½ c (125 ml) margarine
             ¼ c (65 ml) honey
             ½ c brown sugar
Add: 1 egg
Mix: ½ tsp (2 ml) baking soda
             ¼ tsp (1 ml) sea salt (optional)
             1 c (250 ml) whole wheat flour
             ¼ c oat bran
             ¼ c wheat germ or oats
             ½ tsp cinnamon
             ½ tsp nutmeg

1. Add dry mixture to creamed mixture.
2. Add 1 cup of raisins.
3. Drop by teaspoonsful onto ungreased cookie tray.
4. Bake at 375° F (190° C) for about 8 minutes.
5. Leave on cookie tray for 1 minute to cool, then transfer to wire rack to complete cooling.

Fruit Juices

Pineapple/Grapefruit

Cut: one 1-inch (2.5 cm) slice of fresh pineapple. Peel the slice but don't core it. Cut it into strips that will fit into your juicer.

Peel: 1 large grapefruit. Pull apart segments so they fit into your juicer.

Juice: the pineapple and grapefruit together.

Grapefruit/Orange

The proportion I prefer is one large grapefruit to two large oranges. Peel them all and pull apart the segments. Juice them together.

Watermelon

This is an easy, deliciously refreshing juice to make.

Cut: chunks of watermelon to a size that will fit into your juicer. Don't remove the seeds.

Juice: the chunks.

Judy's Chicken Soup Recipe

Ingredients for the Broth
1 chicken
enough water to cover chicken in pot
1 large onion, in chunks
2 large carrots, in large chunks
handful of fresh parsley
1 bay leaf
1 tbsp (15 ml) white vinegar (optional)

1. Remove as much skin from the chicken as you can.
2. Wash chicken under cold running water.
3. Remove the giblets, neck, etc. from the insides if necessary. (You may use them in creating the broth if you wish.)
4. Place the clean chicken in a large pot.
5. Add the onion, carrots, parsley and bay leaf. Cover with water. Add the vinegar if desired. (Using vinegar will help draw out more of the nutrients.)
6. Place the lid on the pot and bring to a boil. Simmer for at least two hours. If you can leave it for longer, you will get more flavorful broth. Check the water level occassionally. Top it up as needed.

Ingredients for the Soup

1 pot of chicken broth
meat from the cooked chicken
4 large carrots, sliced
1 large onion, diced
½ package soup noodles (optional)
1 handful fresh parsley
sage and poultry seasoning to taste
freshly ground pepper to taste

1. When the chicken is thoroughly cooked and you have simmered as long as you want, turn off the heat. Remove chicken from the pot and place on a cutting board.
2. Strain remaining broth. Discard the onion, carrots, herbs and giblets. Dice the meat from the chicken and put it back in the pot with the broth. (Take care that you don't cause the hot broth to splash up on you.)
3. Add the rest of the ingredients. Bring broth to a boil. Simmer until the vegetables are cooked.

This makes a large pot of chicken soup. Keep leftovers in the fridge or freeze in individual portions.

Experiment with other vegetables, herbs and spices.

Sources

Books

Aromatherapy

Black, Penny. *The Book of Potpourri*. New York: Simon and Schuster, 1989.

Duff, Gail. *Natural Fragrances: Outdoor Scents for Indoor Use*. Pownal: Storey Communications, Inc., 1989.

Fischer-Rizzi, Susanne. *Complete Aromatherapy Handbook*. New York: Sterling Publishing Co., Inc., 1990.

Orhbach, Barbara Milo. *The Scented Room*. New York: Clarkson N. Potter, 1986.

Assertion

Alberti, Robert E. & Michael L. Emmons. *Your Perfect Right*. San Luis Obispo: Impact, 1970.

Baer, Jean. *How to Be an Assertive (Not Aggressive) Woman*. New York: Penguin Books USA Inc., 1976.

Fensterheim, Herbert & Jean Baer. *Don't Say Yes When You Want to Say No*. New York: David McKay Company, Inc., 1975.

Smith, Manuel J. *When I Say No, I Feel Guilty*. New York: Bantam Books, 1975.

Children's Books

Barklem, Jill. *The Brambly Hedge Treasury*. London: Harper Collins Publishers Ltd., 1991.

Base, Graeme. *Animalia*. Toronto: Stoddart Publishing Co. Ltd., 1988.

Base, Graeme. *The Eleventh Hour*. Toronto: Stoddart Publishing Co. Limited, 1989.

Bouchard, Dave & Roy Henry Vickers. *The Elders Are Watching*. Tofino: Eagle Dancer Enterprises Ltd., 1990.

Fox, Mem. *Possum Magic*. Norwood: Omnibus Books, 1983.

Hayward, Linda. *Letters, Sounds, and Words*. New York: Platt & Munk, Publishers, 1973.

Hepworth, Cathi. *Antics*. New York: G. P. Putnam's Sons, 1992.

L'Engle, Madeleine. *A Wrinkle in Time.* New York: Dell Publishing Co., Inc., 1962.

Oppenheim, Joanne & Barbara Reid. *Have You Seen Birds?* Richmond Hill: Scholastic–TAB Publications Ltd., 1986.

Colors

Birren, Faber. *Color and Human Response.* New York: Van Nostrand Reinhold Company, 1978.

Gilliatt, Mary. *The Blue and White Room.* New York: Bantam Books, 1992.

Jackson, Carole. *Color Me Beautiful.* New York: Ballantine Books, 1980.

Kobayashi, Shigenobu. *A Book of Colors.* Tokyo: Kodansha International, 1987.

Kobayashi, Shigenobu. *Color Image Scale.* Tokyo: Kodansha International, 1990.

Mella, Dorothee L. *The Language of Color.* New York: Warner Books, Inc., 1988.

Sharpe, Deborah T. *The Psychology of Color and Design.* Chicago: Nelson-Hall, 1974.

Stoddard, Alexandra. *Book of Colors.* New York: Doubleday, 1989.

Walker, Morton. *The Power of Color.* New York: Avery, 1991.

Crafts

Chambers, Anne. *A Guide to Making Decorated Papers.* London: André Deutsch Limited, 1989.

Cosh, Sylvia. *The Crochet Sweater Book.* New York: Crown Publishers, Inc., 1987.

Edwards, Betty. *Drawing on the Right Side of the Brain.* Los Angeles: J. P. Tarcher, Inc., 1979.

Fitzharris, Tim. *The Audobon Society Guide to Nature Photography.* Toronto: Stoddart Publishing Co. Limited, 1990.

Franks, Beth. *Great Gifts You Can Make in Minutes.* Cincinnati: North Light Books, 1992.

Furber, Alan. *Using Calligraphy.* New York: Sterling Publishing Company, Inc., 1992.

Hassel, Carla J. *You Can Be a Super Quilter.* Radnor: Wallace Homestead, 1980.

Lawther, Gail & Christopher Lawther. *Learn Lettering and Calligraphy Step-by-Step*. London: Diagram Visual Information Ltd., 1986.

Nicolaides, Kimon. *The Natural Way to Draw*. Boston: Houghton Mifflin Company, 1969.

Tuckman, Diane & Jan Janas. *The Complete Book of Silk Painting*. Cincinnati: North Light Books, 1992.

Weiss, Daniel, contributing ed. *Reader's Digest Crafts and Hobbies*. Montreal: The Reader's Digest Association, Inc., 1979.

Wiseman, Ann. *Making Things*. Boston: Little, Brown and Company, 1973.

Wiseman, Ann. *Making Things Book 2*. Boston: Little, Brown and Company, 1975.

Creativity

Adams, James L. *The Care and Feeding of Ideas: A Guide to Encouraging Creativity*. Reading: Addison-Wesley Publishing Company, Inc., 1986.

de Bono, Edward. *Serious Creativity*. Toronto: Harper Collins Publishers Ltd., 1992.

SARK. *A Creative Companion: How to Free Your Creative Spirit*. Berkeley: Celestial Arts, 1991.

Stoddard, Alexandra. *Daring to Be Yourself*. New York: Avon Books, 1990.

Thompson, Charles. *What a Great Idea*. New York: Harper Perennial, 1992.

Van Oech, Roger. *A Whack on the Side of the Head*. New York: Warner Books, Inc., 1983.

Wycoff, Joyce. *Mindmapping: Your Personal Guide to Exploring Creativity and Problem-Solving*. New York: Berkley Books, 1991.

Emotional Well-being

Borysenko, Joan. *Minding the Body, Mending the Mind*. New York: Bantam Books, 1987.

Borysenko, Joan. *Guilt is the Teacher, Love is the Lesson*. New York: Warner Books, Inc., 1987.

Chaney, Casey. *Ready, Willing & Terrified: A Coward's Guide to Risk-Taking*. Beaverton: Mocha Publishing Company, 1991.

Hay, Louise L. *You Can Heal Your Life*. Santa Monica: Hay House, 1987.

Jampolsky, Gerald G. *Love is Letting Go of Fear*. Berkley: Celestial Arts, 1979.

Louden, Jennifer. *The Woman's Comfort Book*. San Francisco: Harper, 1992.

Rubin, Theodore Isaac. *The Angry Book*. New York: Collier Books, 1969.

Seligman, Martin E.P. *Learned Optimism*. New York: Pocket Books, 1990.

Gardens

Bremness, Lesley. *The Complete Book of Herbs*. Montreal: Reader's Digest Association Canada Ltd., 1988.

Griffiths, Trevor. *The Book of Classic Old Roses*. London: Penguin Group, 1988.

Keeble, Midge Ellis. *Tottering in My Garden*. Toronto: Oxford University Press, 1988.

Keen, Mary. *The Glory of the English Garden*. London, England: Barrie & Jenkins Ltd., 1989.

Pike, Dave. *Organic Gardening*. Wiltshire: The Crowood Press Ltd., 1990.

Creasy, Rosalind. *The Complete Book of Edible Landscaping*. San Francisco: Sierra Club Books, 1982.

Inspiration

Bachelder, Louise, ed. *On Friendship: A Selection*. New York: Peter Pauper Press, Inc., 1966.

Berkus, Rusty. *Life Is a Gift*. Santa Monica: Red Rose Press, 1982.

Bloch, Douglas. *I Am With You Always*. New York: Bantam Books, 1992.

Brown, Jr., Jackson H. *P.S. I Love You*. Nashville: Rutledge Hill Press, 1990.

de Saint Exupéry, Antoine. *The Little Prince*. New York: Harcourt, Brace & World, Inc., 1971.

Frankl, Viktor E. *Man's Search for Meaning*. New York: Pocket Books, 1984.

Fulghum, Robert. *All I Really Need to Know I Learned in Kindergarten*. New York: Ballantine Books, 1988.

Fulghum, Robert. *Uh Oh*. New York: Vilard Books, 1991.

John-Roger & Peter McWilliams. *You Can't Afford the Luxury of a Negative Thought*. Los Angeles: Prelude Press, 1991.

John-Roger & Peter McWilliams. *Do It*. Los Angeles: Prelude Press, 1991.

Joseph, Michael. *Play Therapy*. St. Meinrad: Abbey Press, 1990.

Kipfer, Barbara Ann. *14,000 Things to Be Happy About*. New York: Workman Publishing Co., 1990.

Lindbergh, Anne Morrow. *Gift from the Sea*. New York: Vintage Books, 1975.

Mundy, Linus. *Slow-down Therapy*. St. Meinrad: Abbey Press, 1990.

Ornstein, Robert & David Sobel. *Healthy Pleasures*. New York: Addison-Wesley Publishing Company, Inc., 1989.

Reps, Paul. *Zen Flesh, Zen Bones*. Rutland: Charles E. Tuttle Co., 1971.

Roads, Michael J. *Simple Is Powerful: Anecdotes for a Complex World*. Tiburon: H. J. Kramer, Inc., 1992.

Stoddard, Alexandra. *Living A Beautiful Life*. New York: Avon Books, 1986.

Thoreau, Henry David. *Walden and Civil Disobedience*. New York: NAL Penguin Inc., 1960.

The Editors of Halo Books. *You Are My Friend*. San Francisco: Halo Books, 1991.

Zimmerman, Bill. *Lifelines: A Book of Hope*. New York: Bantam Books, 1993.

Just for Fun

Adams, Douglas. *The Hitch Hiker's Guide to the Galaxy*. London: Pan Books, 1979.

Armour, Richard. *Twisted Tales from Shakespeare*. New York: McGraw-Hill Book Company, Inc., 1957.

Cassidy, John & B. C. Rimbeaux. *Juggling for the Complete Klutz*. Palo Alto: Klutz Press, 1988.

Eliot, T. S. *Selected Poems*. London: Faber and Faber, 1971.

Keating, Kathleen. *Hug Therapy 2*. Minneapolis: CompCare Publishers, 1987.

Lederer, Richard. *Get Thee to a Punnery*. New York: Dell Publishing, 1988.

Wujec, Tom. *Pumping Ions: Games and Exercises to Flex Your Mind.* Toronto: Doubleday Canada Limited, 1988.

Massage

Carter, Mildred. *Body Reflexology.* New York: Parker Publishing Company, 1983.

Maxwell-Hudson, Clare. *The Complete Book of Massage.* Toronto: Macmillan of Canada, 1988.

Rush, Anne Kent. *Romantic Massage.* New York: Avon Books, 1991.

Music

Birnie, W. A. H., ed. *Reader's Digest Family Songbook.* Montreal: The Reader's Digest Association Canada Ltd., 1970.

Blood-Patterson, Peter, ed. *Rise Up Singing.* Bethlehem: Sing Out Corporation, 1988.

Fowke, Edith. *Sally Go Round the Sun: 300 Songs, Rhymes and Games of Canadian Children.* Toronto: McClelland and Stewart Limited, 1971.

Javna, John. *The Doo-Wap Sing-Along Songbook.* New York: St. Martin's Press, 1986.

Merritt, Stephanie. *Mind, Music and Imagery.* New York: Penguin Books USA, Inc., 1990.

Nelson, Esther L. *The World's Best Funny Songs.* New York: Sterling Publishing Co., Inc., 1988.

Simon, William L., ed. *Reader's Digest Family Songbook of Faith and Joy.* Montreal: The Reader's Digest Association Canada Ltd., 1975.

—*The Best Easy Listening Songs Ever.* Milwaukee: Hal Leonard Publishing Corporation, 1991.

Picture Books

Callaway, Nicholas, ed. *Georgia O'Keeffe: One Hundred Flowers.* New York: Alfred A. Knopf, 1990.

Derry, Ramsay. *The Art of Robert Bateman.* Toronto: Madison Press Books, 1988.

Escher, M. C. & J. L. Locher. *The World of M. C. Escher.* New York: Harry N. Abrams, Inc., Publishers, 1971.

Faulkner, Douglas. *This Living Reef.* New York: Quadrangle/The New York Times Book Co., 1974.

Hines, Sherman. *Extraordinary Light*. Toronto: University of Toronto Press, 1988.

Kallir, Jane. *Grandma Moses: The Artist Behind the Myth*. New York: Clarkson N. Potter, Inc., 1982.

Kurelek, William. *Fields*. Montreal: Tundra Books, 1976.

Langdon, Helen. *Impressionist Seasons*. New York: Universe Books, 1986.

Meier, Leo & Penny Figgis. *Rainforests of Australia*. Sydney: Ure Smith, 1989.

Münz, Ludwig & Bob Haak. *Rembrandt*. New York: Harry N. Abrams, Inc., 1984.

National Film Board of Canada, producer. *Canada/ A Year of the Land*. Ottawa: Queen's Printers, 1967.

Seitz, William C. *Monet*. New York: Harry N. Abrams, Inc., 1960.

Wasserman, Jack. *Leonardo da Vinci*. New York: Harry N. Abrams, Inc., 1984.

Stress Management

Bright, Deborah. *Creative Relaxation*. New York: Ballantine Books, 1979.

Burns, David D. *Feeling Good*. New York: New American Library, 1980.

Charlesworth, Edward A. & Ronald G. Nathan. *Stress Management*. New York: Ballantine Books, 1984.

Clinebell, Howard. *Well Being*. San Francisco: Harper, 1992.

Faelton, Sharon. *Tension Turnaround*. Emmaus: Rodale Press, 1990.

Faelten, Sharon & David Diamond. *Take Control of Your Life*. Emmaus: Rodale Press, 1988.

Groch, Judith, ed. *The Relaxed Body Book*. Garden City: Doubleday & Company, Inc., 1986.

Hanson, Peter G. *The Joy of Stress*. Islington: Hanson Stress Management Organization, 1985.

Harp, David. *The New Three Minute Meditator*. Oakland: New Harbinger Publications, 1990.

Hyman, Jane Wegscheider. *The Light Book*. New York: Ballantine Books, 1990.

Keyes, Jr., Ken. *Taming Your Mind: A Guide to Sound Decisions*. Coos Bay: Love Line Books, 1975.

Kirsta, Alix. *The Book of Stress Survival*. New York: Simon & Schuster, Inc., 1986.

Loehr, James E. & Jeffrey A. Migdow. *Take a Deep Breath*. New York: Villard Books, 1986.

Patel, Chandra. *The Complete Guide to Stress Management*. New York: Plenum Press, 1991.

Peter, Laurence J. *The Laughter Prescription*. New York: Ballantine Books, 1982.

Robinson, Bryan. *Stressed Out?* Dearfield Beach: Health Communications, Inc., 1991.

Tubesing, Donald A. *Kicking Your Stress Habits*. Duluth: Whole Person Associates, Inc., 1991.

Woolfolk, Robert L. & Frank C. Richardson. *Stress, Sanity, and Survival*. New York: New American Library Signet Book, 1978.

Time Management

Eisenberg, Ronni & Kate Kelly. *Organize Yourself!* New York: Collier Books, 1986.

Fanning, Tony & Robbie Fanning. *Get It All Done and Still Be Human*. Menlo Park: Kali House, 1990.

Josephs, Ray. *How to Gain an Extra Hour Every Day*. New York: Penguin Books USA Inc., 1992.

Katz, Patricia. *Getting It Together*. Regina: The Leader-Post Carriere Foundation Inc., 1992.

Silver, Susan. *Organized to Be the Best*. Los Angeles: Adams-Hall Publishing, 1989.

Writing

Bryant, Jean. *Anybody Can Write*. San Rafael: New World Library, 1985.

Capacchione, Lucia. *The Creative Journal*. North Hollywood: Newcastle Publishing Co., Inc., 1989.

Capacchione, Lucia. *The Power of Your Other Hand*. North Hollywood: Newcastle Publishing Co., Inc., 1988.

Goldberg, Natalie. *Writing Down the Bones*. Boston: Shambhala Publications, Inc., 1986.

Killien, Christi & Sheila Bender. *Writing in a Convertible with the Top Down*. New York: Warner Books, Inc., 1992.

Klauser, Henriette Anne. *Writing on Both Sides of the Brain*. San Francisco: Harper, 1987.

Rico, Gabriele Lusser. *Writing the Natural Way*. Los Angeles: J. P. Tarcher, Inc., 1983.

Yoga

Hittleman, Richard L. *Yoga for Physical Fitness*. New York: Warner Books, Inc., 1974.

Volin, Michael & Nancy Phelan. *Yoga Over Forty*. London: Pelham Books, 1965.

Widdowson, Rosalind. *Yoga Made Easy*. London: Hamlyn, 1982.

Exercise Videos

Jane Fonda's Workout Light Aerobics and Stress Reduction Program
Judi Sheppard Missett's Fitness Now
Muscle Building with Charlene Prickett
Rita Moreno: Now You Can

Magazines

Canadian House and Home
Guideposts
International Wildlife
National Geographic
Prevention
Shape
Victoria

Music

Soothing

Calverley – *Celtic Mysteries* (album)
Davol – *Mystic Waters* (album)
Debussy – "Clair de Lune" (composition)
De Koninck – *Music of the Stars* (album)
Halpern, Steven & Georgia Kelly – *Ancient Echoes* (album)
Limor, Gilead – *You Are the Sea* (album)
Pachelbel – "Canon in D" (composition)
Robertson, Kim – *Wind Shadows* (album)

Schubert – "The Little Symphony" (composition)
Sprague – *Ocean Wisdom* (album)
Valentino, Chris – *The Musical Sea of Tranquility* (album)

Uplifting/Invigorating

Bach – "Brandenburg Concertos" (compositions)
Copland – "Rodeo," "Appalachian Spring" (compositions)
Deuter – *Celebration* (album)
Handel – "Water Music," "Royal Fireworks Music" (compositions)
Jones, Michael – *Pianoscapes* (album)
Lynch, Ray – *Deep Breakfast* (album)
Mozart – "Einekleine Nachtmusik" (composition)
Satie – "Three Gymnopedies" (compositions)
Smetana – "The Moldau" (composition)
Wagner – "Ride of the Valkyries" (composition)
Vivaldi – "The Four Seasons" (compositions)
Holst – "The Planets" (compositions)

Relaxation Tapes

Eli Bay's Autogenic Relaxation. The Relaxation Response Ltd., Toronto, Ontario.

Letting Go of Stress. Emmet E. Miller & Steven Halpern, SOURCE, Inc., Stanford, CA.

Ten Minutes to Relax: The Art of Relaxation. Vital Body Marketing Company, Manhasset, NY.

Total Relaxation [subliminal]. Bright Images, Escott International, Inc., Walled Lake, MI.

Thoughts, Ideas and Doodles

Thoughts, Ideas and Doodles